anu

Anu Aggarwal, born and educated in Delhi, shot to fame with her very first Bollywood movie, *Aashiqui*, but then turned her back on films and joined a yogashram. She had a near-fatal car accident that put her in coma for twenty-nine days but from which she miraculously recovered. She took sanyas, but then returned to Mumbai to teach yoga.

anusualbook @ gmail.com

anusual

Memoir of a Girl
Who Came Back from the Dead

Anu Aggarwal

Marcus

Ann mal

love

HarperCollins *Publishers* India

First published in India in 2015 by
HarperCollins *Publishers* India

Copyright © Anu Aggarwal 2015

P-ISBN: 978-93-5029-739-1
E-ISBN: 978-93-5029-740-7

2 4 6 8 10 9 7 5 3 1

Anu Aggarwal asserts the moral right to be identified
as the author of this work.

HarperCollins *Publishers*
A-75, Sector 57, Noida, Uttar Pradesh 201301, India
1 London Bridge Street, London SE1 9GF, United Kingdom
Hazelton Lanes, 55 Avenue Road, Suite 2900, Toronto, Ontario M5R 3L2
and 1995 Markham Road, Scarborough, Ontario M1B 5M8, Canada
25 Ryde Road, Pymble, Sydney, NSW 2073, Australia
195 Broadway, New York, NY 10007, USA

Typeset in 12/15 Goudy Old Style at
SÜRYA

Printed and bound at
Thomson Press (India) Ltd

CONTENTS

Prologue

I nearly died that night. The doctors at Breach Candy Hospital in Mumbai still think it's a miracle I am alive. Alive to tell you about the love I discovered through a ruptured body, a brain bleed, and several incisions of needles and sutures made with surgical thread tied tight.

Change. Resurrection. Revival. Inner transformation. AnuAnew. AnewAnu. AA.

The story of a girl who was broken into a million pieces but is alive to tell the tale of how, like in a jigsaw puzzle, she brought the separated parts together back again. Realignment. Life 2.

But what was the bigger trauma?

Was it facing mobs of fans, each wanting just a piece of me? And flying high lifted into the arms of a few strapping bodyguards, light as a feather?

Or was it being massacred by glass and metal as a

speeding car, in unseasonal heavy rain, made three 360-degree James-Bond kind of turns before crashing on the muddy sands of the Mumbai sea, caving in like a deflated balloon, with me locked in the car?

Or was it getting romantically and spiritually hypnotized by a superyogi, a Paramhamsa, by geometrical images, incandescent light, sound vibrations...and be led to have sex in the forbidden zone?

Love is all there is.

1

Who's That Girl?

Spring, 1987. On a late sunny afternoon, Rick, the jazz drummer, felt his heart pulsate to a new beat. With breathless excitement he looked at her—the girl from another town with an enigmatic air about her. Her wide shoulders defied the old-fashioned Victorian idea equating a woman's beauty with 'sloping slim shoulders'.

On a delicate but assertive tender neckline stood a face with cleverly blended sharp features, a clear jawline with raised cheekbones. Her tender skin texture shone auburn in contrast to the 'Fair is lovely' ideology of India.

Dressed in a multilayered Rajasthani *ghaghra* with a fine-textured, white, full-sleeved t-shirt, she wore heavy silver trinkets that made their own percussion. On the patio in Carter Road, Bombay, he sat and wondered:

'Is she a gypsy, a Sufi, a wanderer? Who is that girl?'

Tall, she carried her curvaceous body straight as a pine. Her laser-straight hair with the sheen of the finest pashmina silk swung around, caressing her erect sinuous back. Her laughter was deep-throttle, a bit boyish. A siren song of freedom. She came across as uninhibited.

I dig you, Anu, was a thought he did not put into words; it was a new association.

In a conversation under the coconut tree on the terrace he found out she was not opinionated. She seemed open to joining a party rather than be a party-pooper. That's cool, Rick would say.

She talked through her deer eyes and spoke little, an attitude that contradicted her bold, forthright gait. He had never seen a prima ballerina with that kind of intensity before. But what struck him most was the rare confidence of the young girl. And the song of Steely Dan, *Hey nineteen! Now we can live together*, started to play in his musical mind.

Goldmist, the colonial house of his friend Aaditya, acquired a brand new, crazy, magical appeal. Butterflies fluttered in the gold-orange light of the twilight zone. Two lost love birds tweeted in perfect harmony.

Frangipani love. Hibiscus love.

It was a friend's wedding that had brought Aaditya to Delhi. The morning after the wedding he was in University of Delhi to meet his friend Gauri. Her corporate father had recently got transferred from Bombay. Dressed in blue jeans, he walked slightly self-consciously in heavy boots. The leather slingbag on his shoulder was a darker shade of his gelled walnut-brown hair.

'Love the way you do fieldwork, the way you question teachers...I am your fan, Anu,' Gauri, a first-year student, my junior in School of Social Work, would admiringly say.

'I want to stand first like you did last year.'

Squinting in the north Indian hot sun, Gauri was energetic as she rushed to me, presenting him proudly: 'Anu! This is Aaditya, my friend from Bombay.'

Gauri's passion for life was unmatched. Trained in Carnatic-style Hindustani classical music, she was also an amazing cook of dosas, but had bad luck with men.

That day, as I stood on the footpath outside the School of Social Work, waiting for a bus to take me home, the bus never came.

Aaditya turned out to be a male of delectable honesty; he had an emotional expressiveness, and a non-macho feel—I knew I was going to spend more time with him. A music lover, Aaditya had just got into photography. With the utmost care he showed me black-and-white pictures he had shot of the Bombay jazz band 'Concoction', where Rick was a drummer.

The pictures came to life on my first evening in Bombay, in Aaditya's colonial house. Rick was in the same white plaid pants with black stripes as in the picture, perhaps his favourite, but the heavy muscular tone was visible now.

I had finally accepted Aaditya's invite. I was on a ten-day holiday before joining a German NGO to work for women's empowerment; they were to start a new programme in Delhi. They had been suitably impressed with my assistance to a Pakistani NGO to better the lives of Muslim women in Jama Masjid and had offered me a job. To furbish my social assistance skills, I volunteered to design a programme for the repatriation of Afghan refugees with the United Nations High Commission for Refugees (UNHCR). This made me one of the privileged students in the School of Social Work to have been offered a job even before I (the highest-score holder in fieldwork, first year) had got my master's degree. I was thrilled, especially since the German NGO offered higher wages than what even the UN did.

Aaditya's artistically pictorial bedroom, next to a blue glass window open to a turbulent sea, contained all I possessed in Bombay. My army green bag that lay on the maroon tiles of the floor had three cotton changes, a book of poems by Pablo Neruda with a couple of dry roses as markers, a couple of silver trinkets, a personal diary, home-made sesame oil, black kohl that Ma had made from burnt almonds, watercolours and art sheets made of vegetable fibre, and the 800 rupees left over from the government scholarship I had received when I graduated (the rest had been used to buy an Indian Airlines ticket for Delhi-Bombay, and a train ticket back to Delhi).

It was a magical evening. On Aaditya's cobble-stoned terrace thrived rare plants, leaves and flowers, the abundance owed to his artist father who watered them fondly each morning. His caring was not a trait restricted only to plants, I would find later, when I got to know his sensitive nature better.

The Bombay sun caught my eye when it descended to the hallucinogenic edge of the sea. The colour in the troposphere moved rapidly from a vague gold to pure orange, and I heard a declaration:

'Come live here.'

And suddenly, a silver lining emerged from the sky and lined the rays of the setting sun in a mesmerizing hue.

Since Basu Da, Aaditya's father, was a film veteran, he received complimentary tickets, and we went to a Satyajit Ray film festival. Aaditya and his girlfriend Sanjana took dutiful turns to show me around, introducing me to their artist friends—painters, writers, musicians, dancers. Bombay was waking up the artist in me. It seemed like a lifetime since I had acted in a play, and theatre was a forgotten word. Though a trained Kathak dancer since I was seven, I did not remember the last time I had tied *ghungroos* on my feet.

For different reasons the week spent in Bombay had been like entering another plane of existence.

A week later, munching fried Bengali lady's fingers in Goldmist, Rick again made sure he sat opposite me. In his tight dark-grey plaid pants and black shoulder-length hair, he wore the attitude of a prince who had lost his empire but maintained a kingly arrogance. His inquisitive eyes had widened, like the drummer was deciding which drum kit to buy.

—Call if you come into town, he said. I am on Woodstock Road, Cuffe Parade.

Apparently, it was only six months ago that the twenty-eight-year-old Rick had had a near-fatal heart attack due to an overdose of cocaine. He had been snorting coke with other band members when he was hit by a sudden bout of breathlessness, and a big-time collapse of senses occurred. In the lover-of-life Rick, fear, panic and desperation took turns as though they competed with each other. His chest pounded at a higher velocity than he could ever beat the snare with his drumsticks.

That was it. Overnight, he got over all addictions. Even caffeine.

Now, as we sat and imbibed pure distilled water on Carter Road, it was very hard for me to imagine him as an addict. But his addictive trait was in-built. Soon he would get addicted to the love of his life—me! And then to peanut butter, which added a few unwelcome calories to his gait.

In Delhi, in a de-addiction clinic, I had counselled patients. Now, in Rick, I found a patient who had kicked the habit beautifully well.

We were perfectly matched, then. And Delhi seemed as far away from Bombay as Timbuktu.

At that time I did not know how improbable this 'chance' happening was: I was bound for Delhi but ended up missing the train by a whisker. Like in a movie, I was left on the station platform, helplessly watching the train disappear.

—Stay Anu, stay, come on, stay!

Rick was keen I stay on in Bombay but the German NGO was waiting, and I was adamant I join them in Delhi as soon as I could. At the station, I bought the next available ticket in the scorching heat of May. Summer season rush ensured the earliest ticket available was only a month later. Rick, who was there at the Victoria Terminus station to see me off, took me with my army bag home; his mother was welcoming:

—You look just like Marilyn Monroe!

And through my direct experience I was led to understand a Tibetan idiom I had read in college:

'It Is All Unknown.'

I stayed in their house on Woodstock Road. A sensational month whisked past,

I was coming to terms with the fast pace of the city. Nobody dressed the way I did. I didn't care if most people thought me strange or a bohemian or whatever. I had seen inside the hearts of people living in gross poverty, I had seen their guileless smiles. And I found the arrogance that money and class provided distasteful.

Working twelve hours a day to better people's lives in Delhi, I had forgotten my artisitic side—like acting in theatre and dance, my last foray being in Ananda Shankar's East meets West troupe. Now the next level of life exploration had begun. Social service, I decided, would have to wait. Little did I know how my social work would weave itself into the glitter of glamour.

I was getting ready to write to Kelucharan Mahapatra and pursue Indian classical dance through the Odissi classical dance form.

But when the moment came, Rick baba started to weep like a baby.

—Please don't go...go later.

In my life, I had never seen a grown man cry—for me. That, and his irresistible caring, melted me. Rick's generous heart had captivated me. I saw my urgency for Odissi dance take a back seat. OK. Later.

And that 'later' never came.

The next month, on a rainy day, in a grotesquely crowded Western line of suburban railways, at Churchgate station, a talent scout spotted me and exclaimed:

'You are a model!'

I was against glorifying a product. Advertising it in an exaggerated way, promising it is more than it actually is, went against my grain. In addition, I had grown up spoilt with the feeling:

I don't have to use my face, I have a mind that works.

Since there were no modelling agencies like Elite in

India then, the advertising agencies began to look for me. Rick saw my reluctance to take their calls. They followed me like a dog to a bone.

'Hear them out, just see what they have to offer. What have you got to lose? The choice to say "yes" or "no" is yours.'

I agreed to meet them.

To do away with the advertising brigade, in our first meeting with the agency Mudra, I quoted an outlandish price, way higher than what the top model got then.

I was stunned to have them agree. In the advertisement: foam bubbles of a pink soap highlighted the transparency of my clear, tawny skin. People saw the well-distributed Godrej Marvel soap advertisement, and asked the same question Rick had when he first saw Anu:

—'Who's that Girl?'

And with the first advertisement, irrevocably, I had become one of the most sought-after and highly-paid models. It was a time in India when the term 'supermodel' was just being coined. *Society* magazine in 1988 had me dressed in my tight blue jeans on the cover, with the title 'India's first supermodel'. One of the first models the magazines vied to converse with, interview and feature.

It was anybody's guess as to how, within just six months of her arrival in the city, an unknown young lass with zero family credentials, perhaps still not of a mature age, had tasted public success.

Inasmuch as it had people in awe of me, it raised jealousy and criticism as well. But my social work background helped me stay grounded.

In my silly uppity way I was not looking for it, but earning money meant I could get off the diet I had followed since my start in Bombay—I could afford more than just an apple and salted peanuts for lunch.

And not only did my rent get looked after but I could buy toothpaste and cream too. I could do away with the Blind School that offered me a counselling job with the kids and quarters to stay in, but where I would be on call all day to a lady patron who drank the finest whisky at night in a plush leather-and-chrome bedroom and pretended to be concerned about poverty during the day. Females can fake it better than males.

I took the plunge.

I explored the new city, India's Big Apple.

During the day I walked around Lion Gate, checked out the Bombay stock exchange, marvelled at the lush green old trees, saw happy slum kids on the street playing ball. The Bombay suburban railway, with its more than seven million commuters each day, was fun. I felt a part of the bustling crowd, eager to strike a balance between desire and survival.

What was an unbelievable boon was that though I was in crowded train compartments, still my buttocks didn't get pinched, or breasts rubbed 'mistakenly' by males, like it happened in Delhi. But people stared. Was it because I wore my 'wanderer' *ghaghra*, my head covered like a Muslim's? In any case, with the unwavering attention that made a grab for me on the local Bombay train, I felt like I was wearing a wedding gown at a funeral ceremony.

I drove by the adorable Queen's Necklace on Marine Drive by night; I could see the midnight blue head of the queen decorated with glittering stars, her wearing the necklace of little bulbous drops. Magical.

Since I had no patrons in the business of glamour, no parents in the city, was new in Bombay, perhaps that led to my being labelled with the tags, 'Mysterious girl; Enigma.'

And what stayed as a mystery was how, in a country that in the 1980s believed only 'fair' was 'lovely', perhaps some complex hangover from the British Raj, my tanned skin colour had become such a rage.

Later it would be used as a trump card to describe my uncanny success: 'In spite of her dark complexion...Anu has made it.' More than getting flattered, I hoped the young girls in schools would get fascinated, inspired, and never again be ashamed of having dark skin. Or anything you are naturally born with. Colour doesn't matter, your skills do.

Woman, you are a goddess!

In the dripping wet Bombay monsoon, it was far from my imagination that I would turn into a style icon soon. That I would get plastered on hoardings, wallpapers, calendars, splashed on covers of magazines, and anything else that came in the name of entertainment.

The first time I saw the large picturesque frame, I was stunned. It was disbelief, shock, a bolt out of the blue. There I stood, in a massive hoarding, in a blue sari with a spaghetti string top, eyes lowered, cheekbones prominent, silky brownish/black hair falling straight like the line of the horizon behind wide shoulders. Is that me?

I remembered that morning, when I got dolled up before the shoot.

'Micky, can you make her look fair?'

The Italian wife of one of the top Indian photographers was surprisingly more Indian than the natives. She stood and glared disapprovingly at me, but the make-up artist did not even give her as much as a side glance; he continued to apply the make-up base on my face.

'Bitch. Look at her coming and belittling you. Oh these menopausal wives and their jealousy of young models.'

Behind thick glasses, Micky muttered, bending waist down to apply the mauve eye shadow. The untimely reaction of the photographer's wife is a shock, a bummer, on my first shoot. Perhaps prejudice was born out of that: colour. White or black. Blue or grey. Yellow or...does it frigging matter?

That morning, there were a series of difficulties. Chembur? What is that? Name of a person? Oh, oh, I see, a place! Push, shove your way in—love the Bombay local trains. Oh, there run two lines, two parallel train tracks, and lo and behold! Chembur is not on the same line as Churchgate I have just got familiar with.

Time-bound by habit, I breathe punctuality. I have done it, lived like that in Delhi. No reason why I shouldn't aim for that here. Hey, you be you.

Can't believe I made it. Ali's studio is a ten-minute walk from the Chembur station. It's monsoon time in Bombay, and watercoats and umbrellas add colours, a flowery lustre, to the pitch-grey sky. Am I a model? Oh, no! Pray, tell me that's not true. Time was, this reality was not even a preferred dream, if not a nightmare. From early adolescence, if there was one thing I abhorred, it was fakeness. Pretentiousness was always unattractive. And I suspected the glamour world oozed it. I had shied away from it.

Now with my first shoot I was to become a part of the same glamour world. It would pay my rent, but the reaction of the photographer's wife had been discouraging. Was she jealous that at the dining table that morning, as we had coffee and sandwiches, Ali did not take his eyes off me? But he is a photographer, I told myself, he would observe the piece he would turn into a fine art form. Sticky jealousy. Or was it prejudice?

At this moment I was in a taxi on the Peddar Road flyover. In Bombay, finding a roof over my head had been the hardest. I was returning after seeing a PG dig and going to inspect the next. I was facing the brunt of daring to be a young girl alone—unacceptable in the late eighties in India. It raised questions and eyebrows. I was an object of undesired suspicion, like I was a ripe mango that could be a bit rotten inside.

On Napean Sea Road, a Gujarati landlady had scrutinized me from head to toe. Her disdain was evident. She asked what I did and when I replied, she said directly,

—We don't give to models...and...where is your father?

—In Delhi, I answered. A simple, straightforward, honest reply to what I thought was a simple, direct question.

I was still reeling under the rudeness of Madame M's gesture when she slammed the door on an expectant, needy young face.

In January 1988, Daniel Mascarus, the Portuguese fashion photographer, insisted, for the umpteenth time, that we do a shoot. We were driving up the spectacular Walkeshwar road, listening to 'Something About You' by the band Level 42. I was admiring the Parsi fire temple and did not pay attention to his repetitive refrain.

'You are getting my goat,' he said, exasperated.

—Oh yeah? What about my cows you've been getting on all evening? I fluttered my lashes with the retort.

He broke into an open laugh, and so did I.

The next day I was at the Jehangir Art Gallery where I had gone to look at a display of watercolour paintings, as that was the medium I used to doodle in. On this windy day numerous folds of my billowing Rajasthani *ghaghra* filled the gallery hallway.

—Wow, Anu, you walk like a model! You will sashay down the fashion ramp, Sharmila, the choreographer, beamed joyously.

It turned out I was chosen to walk the ramp because I had a natural model's walk. It was not that I first became a model and then learnt the appropriate model walk.

Sharmila's gregarious laugh was infectious. It melted any remaining resistance or resentment I had for the fashion and beauty world. I had shot a commercial already, so why not walk the talk now? And get paid for it? If nothing else, it will be an experience, I argued in an attempt to convince myself. Just one show. Like I did one play with a particular theatre group, I could do just one show and the experience need not be repeated. Catwalk.

The next thing I knew I was in London walking the ramp in a chalet just outside of London, and had a duke hit on me! Till then I knew of the duke only when the Duke of Edinburgh award was given to me for elocution when I was eleven years old, a schoolgirl then. And now this!

My ticket to London, UK, was paid for. The thrill of flying alone, working and earning in pounds marked the next step on my evolutionary curve. Little did I know then that this was to open doors—that international modelling offers would come in appreciation of my auburn skin. This was balm on the wounds of my daredevil solo living in India in the late eighties, and the difficulties thereof. I was stunned and delighted in one breath. Having international currencies, pounds and dollars in my purse, was a new thrill. I had a blast.

I walked the ramp on a cruise from Norway to Mexico via Germany, balancing on stilettos being the hardest what with the high choppy sea. Modelled for a five-page fashion shoot for the Greek *Cosmopolitan* magazine. Catwalked the ramp at the Marriott Hotel, New York, only to have my bag picked later at a Macy's sale on the day I was to fly back to India. My small purse with all earned dollars gone but what was the worst was losing my passport! I found out what a liability an Indian passport was—it took forever to get a new one.

Got chosen to rub a bottle of Schweppes Indian Tonic on my cheek by an American agency located in Paris. And fell in love with Africa in Kenya, where, after the fashion show, we were taken to a barbeque dinner where I sat through a twelve-course meal, more interested in the golden-red African mud than tasting crocodile and buffalo meat. When off duty on the Indian ramp, rather than baking and tanning in the sun by the pool of the hotel as other models would, I preferred to tour remote spiritually-inclined places such as the Aurobindo ashram in Pondicherry.

I had the most glorious year-and-a-half, knowing little that soon I was to be thrust into a different kind of stardom.

2

Stardom

It had all begun just a year ago. It was at Sea Rock Hotel, Bandra, at a common friend's luncheon, that I chanced to meet Mahesh Bhatt.

'You are a star!'

The art filmmaker of the 'sensible' kind loved me from the start.

'In the galaxy?' I humoured him.

I was sorry to disappoint him but in that instant I was reminded of the time I was working with abandoned Muslim mothers in a Jama Masjid slum. A well-known NGO from Karachi was visiting. To highlight the 'social effects of media-entertainment' they showed video clips from epic films. One of them was a scene from *Devdas*, where the hero hits the head of the female lead, Paro, with a stone and mutters lines worthy of a male chauvinistic pig, when she refuses his moves.

It was not just the women locked within the confines of the Jama Masjid slums who faced male atrocities at home—I was influenced, too. At age eighteen, I was dazed by how media and entertainment could generate hype, create mass hysteria, and encourage a regressive sense of fashion, taste and style.

In the commercial cinema of the late eighties, the typical lead heroine was a rich father's brat, who shook her boobies and booty for a couple of song-and-dance numbers. She was a kind of a bimbo, not fit for much else other than being a physical object evoking lust and desire in men, and dependent on the father/lover to feed her and lead her ahead in life.

'There is nothing in Hindi films that interests me. I don't even watch them. Not interested.'

I was equally certain.

'Call me if you change your mind.'

I won't. I didn't. Of course not. But thank you, anyway.

It was a hot tropical December in Bombay in 1989—at most one needed a cotton scarf in the evening. I was in the city to pack up. Pay my dues and wind up. I was to go back to Paris. To Laurent and the modelling agency MG that had classified me as a model with a 'special look'. This was a huge compliment as 'special' meant being from an unidentifiable origin. I could be mulatto, South American, Mexican. It meant I had the look of the world, an international appeal.

I received a call. My absence in Mumbai had been a pressing problem for the filmmaker. In the year since we first met, he had written a script.

—*Aashiqui* is based on your life, Anu, will you play Anu Varghese, the lead, in it?

He admitted matter-of-factly. He spoke really fast. He seemed to mean what he said.

My gaze travelled from the phone to the window, the large peepul tree sheltering it. I was bidding adieu to my home for over a year. This movie director approaching me, this Bollywood offer, seemed totally out of synch. A film based on my life? Hah, what does he know about me? Aha, my interviews to a few tabloids—is he basing the story on journalistic reports that at best are callously half-baked...It sounds banal. Can't be true...Since he knows of my resistance to acting in Hindi films, this must be his way to home in...

'If you don't act I will reconsider making the movie...Besides, no other actress has the sensibility to play this role.'

Wow! Thanks for the compliment, I thought without putting it in words.

In a low and barely audible voice I heard myself mutter,

'I will call you back.'

That afternoon in the Portuguese-style bungalow of Elaine Bocarro, on Mount Mary Road, Bandra, I reminisced:

Each magical morning in Paris, the boulangerie below

my building provided freshly-baked hot croissants. Le Paris was magical, what with art being sold on the streets in the form of black-and-white pictures, coffee a local hallucinogen one drank several times a day, the Parisian unabated openness to female nudity refreshing, especially for someone who had grown up in Delhi, where the woman was always held somehow responsible for inviting that unsavoury male attention, eve-teasing.

In Europe I found I could change identity easily, as the common male reaction was:

'You mulatto? Or Spanish? Mexican, perhaps?'

There was a polite curiosity expressed in broken English, in a heavy French accent.

They were magnetically pulled to me, like I was the most delectable Beaufort cheese—with a nice smell of milk, butter and honey, or something. And of course, I was more than flattered.

In India, shamelessly, the aunty-types held that at best I was 'attractive'; to be 'beautiful' I would have to whitewax the colour of my skin. And as I grew up, the rebel in me became more stubborn about flaunting the taint of my tawny skin. Accept what you are born with, naturally, being my feeling.

Carrying the French magazine *Le Point*, that had my mug with the Schweppes Indian Tonic bottle rubbing against my cheek, I had just returned from Paris.

Anu Varghese was a strangely compelling character to play: the orphan teen, born out of wedlock and abandoned at birth, is raised in a Catholic orphanage. The simple, introverted young lass grows up dreaming of love, sustenance, and a place in society. But above all she seeks 'to stand on her own two feet and become somebody and find herself':

Main apne pairon pe khadi hona chahti hoon
Main khud kuchh banna chahti hoon
Mera apna kuchh paana chahti hoon

Now this phrase, this admonition of the lead actor, is why I finally got lured into saying 'yes' to the movie. It came from my belief that instead of being dependent on the man, girls need to be independent first. And then, it would help do away with the lies and false game-playing in a relationship.

Aashiqui was a love story—the craziness of youthful love between a homeless parentless orphan girl and a singer-guitarist. A romantic tale that believed, and claimed:

'Love makes life live.'

'Romance' made me think of Laurent the art dealer and restaurateur in Paris who had aroused me—and I was to hurry back for him, as promised. The particular arrondisement his building, built in old French architecture, stood in, ran alongside a river. The last month of our courtship saw Laurent and me bond. He showed me Le Paris and France the way I had never seen it before—it was ecstasy. I, a teetotaller, got introduced to the delicacy of French wine. French rave. Chalets in cornfields, romance in the European countryside. Our first month together had been magical. One month of courting over, an association and closeness had developed; we lay together that partially diffused morning and watched the gentle flow of water in the shimmering river. And the entire day went by.

After being caressed and coddled, my light brown body glistened in its bareness, sparkling like gold in the evening light. Lying on the pastel green sheet, I had felt calm and content.

The modelling agency MG for 'models with special looks' is what I had in mind when I told Laurent, 'I'll be back', before I boarded the British Airways Paris-Bombay flight.

In appreciative Paris, my release had been unmatched—I belonged there. Enough to consider buying a plot of land there—and never ever leave. And then of course there was Laurent...

As it was, I was not keen to act in Bollywood. Their childish film structure, with cartoon-like heavy emotional baggage, made me laugh. The dances were embarrassing to watch; they had nothing of the fine art of either traditional Indian or Western dance. Their design sense for costumes left a lot to be desired. There was no passion for real fashion, no chic style. Alas!

Do I choose French modelling and love? Or take the call of Bollywood? Where the radical role of a young girl was an opportunity to use entertainment in a progressive way?

I was not sure.

And under the hay roof of Elaine's bungalow, with the raw plushness of the old babul tree outside my bedroom window, I tried to avoid the persuasive calls of the director.

I returned to see Mahesh a couple of days later on his shoot. He sat on a white plastic chair, with a couple of people sitting hopefully at his feet, like he was about to distribute the rarest of candies. I would know them later as his *chamchas*, including the hero of the movie.

Suitably pleased at my arrival, he immediately began to fuss over me.

The producer and the crew looked at me in dubious-curious anticipation. Who does she think she is? Shaking her straight mahogany-black hair, in torn denim jeans, a pouch stretching around the waist, and a small leather haversack? She does not look like a heroine, is not even a movie star yet, and is playing hard to get? When any of the existing top stars are ready, willing, and waiting to be signed?

But the curtain of inquisitive doubt was tinged with the admiration they had for Anu the hot lissome supermodel. In their puckered lips, sipping masala chai, hid a desire—a curious, luscious longing for familiarity.

'Another round of tea?' Saying this, the director signalled for a chair.

I saw the worker boys on a film set for the first time, and my thoughts went to the slum-dwellers I'd worked with. I felt an instant warmth and affection tinge my heart.

On seeing me his soft face had lit up in an intense golden hue—I realized it was the expression of a person who, having lost all hope, finds his favourite ring of gold again. In the last few days, he had kept calling, waiting for me to confirm I was acting in the movie, and I kept saying—I will call you back.

Mahesh welcomed me with aplomb; he obviously didn't know I had come prepared to say 'no'.

I was armed with my best arrow—

'I'm considering doing the film, but I have to return to Paris and since Hindi films have a reputation of taking forever to complete, I am sorry...'

Pat came his question—When?

—Now.

No, he said, he meant when is the latest I could go to Paris.

—Before the next season of haute-couture begins; it is winter right now, so before the spring collection, I stated clearly.

The response rotated mid-air and hit him. A bullet of an answer from him:

—We will complete in three months. For sure.

To my 'that's unbelievable' look, he nodded, affirming 'No-BS (bullshit), I mean it.'

He says he will complete the film fast...Now what?

My next arrow shot a list of dos-and-don'ts. This included almost all that I was uncomfortable doing—in 1989 the fashion in Indian films was desperately behind that in New York, Paris and London. The character is sympathetic. And the way I see it, it is without glitz or glamour. So I will not, playing the role, wear fake eyelashes or pink rouge to highlight and display the rose of my cheeks. Or wear white base to look 'fair'. Or wear falsies to enhance breasts, which were then deliberately shaken in item numbers. Or wear navel-revealing frilly skirts. No fake smiles. Or entice with a damsel-in-distress look of a single girl dependent on her father or brother. Curling or cutting hair in steps, the fashion adorned by actresses in India, I will not do. I will let my normal dead-straight, all-in-one-length hair remain. And it will be tied tight in a ponytail. And yes, I will have my own fashion designer.

I was waiting for him to disagree. His eyes had widened considerably. His breath stopped for a second. His mouth was open in expectation.

—Anything you want, Anu!

A ray of light entered my cranium. Behind the pearl earrings pinned on my ears I heard:

'Do It. JUST DO IT.'

The next day, in an old dilapidated house in Chembui village, Bandra, I lip-synched the song:

Jaane jigar jaane man…jaanam jaane jaan jaanam jaane jahaan—

The hero of the film, Rahul, sang proclamations of first love, swore death if not togetherness.

On hearing this promise, for me the actor, the air stopped circulating, water stopped flowing, the world blurred out. So engaged was I, all I could see any more was him, just the hero, whose name did not even matter anymore. Gushes of first love. I repeated the exact same lines, confirming the age-old Romeo-Juliet madness. Looked him in the eye.

My first shot.

But it was the strangest thing to pretend to sing an already recorded song that blared from junk old-fashioned speakers. Lip-synch honey, pretend, enter the fake and delicious world of Bollywood. Amen!

In those days the ad filmmakers had naturally upturned noses, they lived a life of transparency. Art and university education clapped hands in advertising. On the other hand, the grungy, raw, low-literacy-level lot involved in movies clicked cash deals under the table. There was almost zero transparency. Obviously, the advertising and movie worlds did not see eye to eye.

So when I signed a film there were friendly brows crossed. The jingling world of advertising jangled a bit.

—Anu, are you sure? Want to deal with that squad of goons?

Ad guru Prahlad Kakkar, a close friend, raised his bushy eyebrows, laughed in mockery.

The film business then was known for its unprofessionalism, was believed to be ruled by underworld dons.

A young orphan girl born in the worst of circumstances, makes it superbig—my role emphasized women's empowerment, independence, success, was enough reason for me to play it. That's that.

Preparation for my role began. Traits of Anu Varghese, my character, came into play. What could an orphan girl abandoned by her parents and condemned by the dean of the orphanage feel? Helplessness, shyness, I gathered. Does she dream of a home? Sexual intimacy? But of course she must dream of making it on her own, since she does not want to be a burden on anybody.

What is my method of acting?

Well, darling, it is the method in the starkness, a poke in the invisible, a beam of light in the darkness. Jokes apart, I work from deep inner consciousness. So first you take in the image, the essence—the overall view includes even what other actors are doing, and not just your part. And then let yourself feel as the part. Then let what the feeling evokes take over.

While the shooting was on, I was given the space, as an actor, to experiment. Mahesh let me play the role my way, questioning my logic but then agreeing to my reasoning. Improvise impromptu. Perhaps the experienced art-film director saw Anu get under the skin of Anu Varghese.

He'd laugh encouragingly, call me a 'One-Take Artist'.

The director did not have to chew nails in nervous anticipation for me to act in my debut film. Right after my very first take, he shouted 'OK' happily. This then followed for all the other scenes.

'It was *Love in the Time of Cholera*, the book by

Gabriel Garcia Marquez that you gave me, and I studied for the role, that helped.' I teased him too.

The air rotated with warmth of the softest silk pashmina, and the shoot was marked by trust.

By the time the film reached completion, in a period of four months, I had gone through a massive personal upheaval. In a shoot one just turned the face—left profile turned right profile. Modelling, even though it brought international fame, did not sustain my interest anymore—the creativity was missing. Acting a role, shooting a movie, had been an electrifying experience. Walking down the ramp came nowhere close to this. There I flaunted a designer dress, whereas here I wore a dress the character I played would. I made visible emotions—of love, hate, despair, fear, happiness, expectation, sadness. I drew from the deep hidden feelings inside me.

As an actor you convey an idea, a feeling, and not just a walk. It is way more than being just a suitable physical size of a made-up fashion doll.

One night:

Robert Sethi, who was in India setting up the Indian office of MG Stanley, took me dancing. We drove in his white Mercedes all the way to south Bombay to the popular nightclub Ecstasy, where we shook more than a bouncy leg all night. Then when he came to drop me back home, in Juhu, I discovered I had lost the house key.

Standing in the darkness of the third floor with no floor lights on, I vehemently searched each nook and cranny of my Saatchi bag. No luck. I did not possess a duplicate key and my landlady Rita was out of town. Could the wooden door swallow me into the apartment? Or how would it be if I disappeared in the wall and appeared magically on the side of my bed inside? Alas! No such thing happened. Life is tough.

Drawn to Eastern mysticism and philosophy, Robert laughed and said,

'What does not have to, does not happen.'

Exactly like my older brother Anurag, Robert came up with these sizzling one-liners; they were both brilliant, both chose to study finance over anything else.

We drove all the way back to the Taj Mahal Hotel, Colaba. In the mischievous purity of the star of Venus in the dawn, he responsibly checked me into a room, caringly gave me orange juice for breakfast, decently tucked me in bed, and did not try any sexual stunts of the normal male kind. That was the day when in my mental diary his status changed—from 'friend' to 'best friend'.

And then, a few months later, *Aashiqui* was released.

Excessive fame is a motherf*cker.

A kind of a corny helplessness was scaring the living daylights out of me—

I mean: Now? What do I do?

I am what they call a 'star'.

My life had flipped sides without my permission. I personally did not mind that copious adulation, for sure, but after the release of *Aashiqui* an indoor life followed. When not shooting or at a media event I was home, like a lioness trapped inside a cage.

It became even harder to rent a house—the 'star' rents are higher always. Ma offered to buy me a place. I declined, I was trying to prove I was independent—I rented a flat in Worli. Secure inside, in three bedrooms and a large hall, within the four walls and the ceiling, this was the only private place left for me.

Next, I locked all those expectant and respectful producers out—most of whom were twice my age or more. Producers whose gold chains clattered as they expectantly tapped the main door of my hiding abode. Producers balancing heavy suitcases filled with bundles of cash in their awe-filled hands, full of hope that they would convince me, sign me up for a flick.

I took a few months off.

In my whirl of study and social work, I had hardly had the time or inclination even to watch movies. I loved acting in the theatre but even that had taken a backseat. I bought a movie player. I started to educate myself. I saw four to five films a day. Old Hollywood classics, comedies, films of masters like Kurosawa and Fellini, festival films, you name it.

Theatre to films: From overdoing things, shouting the dialogue in a loud voice, and slightly exaggerated body postures on stage to underdoing—in a close-up, a camera catches even a slight quiver of a lip.

Stardom proved devastating for my personal life. In the hot summer of Bombay in 1991, for the umpteenth time, I broke up and again patched up with Rick—his mother's friends had commented slyly on the 'numerous' men Anu 'chewed' and 'spat out'—as presented by the media. I found the young rebel in me clutch my privacy like raw diamond—I never defended myself. I stayed cooped up, felt it was degrading to make time for those who threaded the nasty tales. This kind of non-diplomacy didn't go in my favour.

Insecure with my success, Rick seemed to believe a lot of the fabricated musings of tabloids about me. Doubt dropped red ink in the otherwise clear water of Rick's mind. Questioning my morality, Rick turned inconsolable to any answers I gave: suspicion, doubts, and arguments withered the tender soil of an otherwise quiet, trusting relationship.

It was an awesomely difficult time. Who is this Anu Aggarwal the press talks about? It certainly is not Me. On the phone, appalled by some nasty press clipping, Ma said,

'They don't know you.'

That helped.

I had a family of three people—all were headstrong and had above-average intelligence. Due to our close bonding, we supported each other's decisions even when we did not appreciate them. In crucial times in life we were sure we would be there for the other. But for any of them, accompanying me to a shoot was out of the question. They were busy doing stuff they wanted to; they were not awe-struck by glamour, not pulled enough by money, nor attracted to the blitz or glitz of stardom.

I would have to live alone, work alone, and manage domestic affairs as well as bank accounts, taxes, lawyers, and shooting schedules alone. That in a country and in a rough, disorganized entertainment business which, in the early 1990s, raised a moralistic eyebrow at 'a girl alone'.

With no family around, Rick was the only one I could turn to for support. At least he knew me, I thought. I was wrong. Our relationship was already in the gloom of cheerlessness. *Kissa paise ka*. Money, that's where problems began—I'd got a whopping sum for my first modelling assignment. Rick asked I convert my Hong Kong Bank account, single so far, into a joint one. So he could withdraw cash whenever he needed to?

His audacity was as shocking as his 'new' bitchiness about fellow musicians. Where was the 'brotherhood-of-man' principle he touted when I first met him? And the joint account thing? That was outrageous. In my family each person had a separate bank account. It was taken for granted that it was the prerogative of the account-holder to change the status from single to double if they so desired. That Rick asked, struck me as odd; he was out of line. Besides, he was a 'spendthrift', as weak in holding his wallet full as he was in filling it. Seeds of doubt crept up in my mind: does Rick expect me to support him?

He was the apple of my eye, the sugar in my plum, I'd have done it for him regardless of any misgivings. But the rational part of my mind told me it was time to act sensibly...I refused Rick access to my bank account.

Guavas pink and bright on the surface get rotten inside due to a tiny green slippery worm.

Our ripe relationship never flipped its feathers again.

The nail fitted in by the hammer of stardom did its job. Media reports accusing 'sex bomb' Anu of outrageous flirtations, of her debatable promiscuity towards both sexes, did it. A deathly virus of Anu Aggarwal's questionable morality spread far and wide, clouding all else in her life. Sex sells. I felt like a scapegoat. The virus had entered Rick's trustworthy nerves too.

Thank you, media. Thanks, stardom.

And so went the man I came closest to marrying...ever...The only guy I took home to Delhi, the first and the last I ever presented to Amma.

A year after *Aashiqui* I was flooded with offers, specially for New Year stage shows abroad. Most of the shows looked dubious, such as one by an Indian in Toronto whose only drive was to make money (nothing wrong with that but the show should be worth each cent of the promoter's money) and who lacked any sense of class and style—I was not available for them. But a show in Kenya seemed interesting and I was considering it when, one day, my doorbell rang. I opened the door to an unrecognizable girl who was balancing her petite frame on flat Kolhapuri chappals. Without make-up, her hair tied in a plait, she was dressed in a no-frills, cotton *salwar kameez*.

—Anuuuuu!

Her excited exclamation was in a familiar voice. A cloud of vague recollection passed above my head, and I said, 'Victoria?'

The last I saw her, Victoria had curled, puffed, gelled auburn hair. The longest of long high heels balanced her form. The twenty-two-year-old professional flamenco dancer had come to India to perform at the Taj Mahal Hotel, Delhi.

Victoria narrated the following story:

After her performance in the hotel, during the two free days she had before her next show in Taj Mahal Hotel, Bombay, she visited an ashram in Rishikesh.

There she met a swami, they both were bowled over by each other, she never went back.

A clandestine courtship lasted eight months. They planned a secret marriage. Her Spanish mother, also a flamenco dancer, flew to London, and prepared for a Catholic Christian wedding in a church. A honeymoon room was booked, it was to be decked with flowers.

If all had gone according to plan, Victoria and the swami, after their marriage in a church and a honeymoon in Spain, would have returned to India, he in his *dhoti* and she in *salwar kameez*, and lived happily ever after in the ashram, carrying on clandestinely as before. Nobody needed to be told. Nobody needed to know.

All air reservations made, suites booked, guests invited by Victoria's mother and brothers. All ready, waiting for the bride and groom.

The swami lost it two days before flying to London. He fell seriously ill. Maybe it had to do with his sanyasi's vow of celibacy. The bride-to-be Victoria became a nurse to her ailing groom-to-be, by the Ganges in Rishikesh.

The swami went into a stupor; Victoria sat by his bed tending to him. She believed all would be well after he recovered. Only the wedding plan had failed, but that too could happen later.

All day, all night, the swami slept. Maybe the fatigue of his own lies in the last eight months finally got to him. His Spanish love affair in the ashram had been under utmost secrecy. Nobody had even suspected it.

Finally, when he came to after a week, guilt had got the better of him. He blamed Victoria for his serious celibate life going astray. For his not advancing towards nirvana, as she had wrapped him in a delicate feminine web. For him to return to his monastic order vows meant that she had to go. He forcefully threw her out of the ashram.

As a hysterical Victoria sat by the bank of the Ganges, an angel appeared in human garb and led her to Vipassana meditation, saying it would cure her grief.

It did.

And I had sat glued. Vipassana, with which I had so far been unfamiliar, intrigued me. I shelved a plan to visit Africa. I had been baffled, what with this unexpected sudden stardom. Victoria and I booked ourselves for a ten-day course of Vipassana, starting the next morning. And drove overnight to Kutch for it.

Apart from following the five precepts of 'no cheating, no lying, no stealing, no sexual misconduct and no intoxication', we promised to observe silence.

My first course was really tough. How do you sit without moving, without speaking, for eight hours a day? That too in the same place, in the same posture, on the floor? In meditation I deviously hacked plots of escape. Run away! The fact that I had committed and signed for ten days needled me. If I ran away I would be a failure.

I am not born to lose.

I lasted.

After the initial resistance of three days, on the seventh day I felt my entire body vibrate. Each cell in the body, every molecule, rang a bell, sang a song, and danced. The rhythm of movement of each subatomic particle was unique. A rainbow appeared.

I returned on 3 January 1991 to the city, and reported in time for shooting—a month ago I had signed to play the typical, slightly silly booby lass, Fanny, a Portuguese from Goa, in Rakesh Roshan's movie, *King Uncle*. A character totally different from the introverted orphan of *Aashiqui*, it was a creative, fun role.

Apart from *King Uncle*, I completed *Ghazab Tamasha*, a family drama where I played a young slum girl. I had hardly had time to rest when, at the start of 1992, Mani Ratnam's office called. Would I consider doing a movie with him? Play the powerful role of an underworld queen, Chandralekha?

Wow! Have you ever seen an oracle dance—this was one time I got up and started to dance. Wow! Mani, the wonder craftsman? Calling me, who is just a film old. Even the superior advertising folks, who disdained Bollywood, were in awe of Mani—does he have four hands instead of two?

In Mani's film, *Thiruda Thiruda*, the shooting locations were at least three hours away from Chennai. Mani shot most close-ups in twilight, or in the fresh glow of dawn. He was an immaculate craftsman. One who cleared the soil of every debris, each minor stone, even before he planted the seed, leave alone basking in the shade of what the tree will grow up to look like.

It was a pleasure to watch him turn roll into reel. And we had the same ultimate goal—to produce a pure spectacle for the audience. Entertain them, give them solace from their routine lives.

And the south Indian film crew knew what they

were doing. Like the make-up man in his simple white cotton *dhoti*; each morning, no matter what time we started, he was in my hotel room on the dot. The red *tilak* on his forehead said he had bathed and prayed to the goddess of beauty before he came.

And the *dhoti*-clad make-up man was more progressive than most of his Bollywood counterparts; he was up-to-date with the latest international make-up products.

The team was on red alert so far as the director went; they worshipped him. And they were completely flummoxed by my 'un-heroine like' way—they saw me chainsmoke Camel cigarettes with the 'mood ring' on my finger, and report on time on shoot without a 'mother' or family/*chamchas* paraphernalia. The notion that Bollywood heroines can't dance was prevalent in the 250 dainty dancers on the set. This was the suspicion of the choreographer, too.

But on the second day of shooting he walked up to me, his teeth jutting out of his beard on a tan face:

'This will be the song of the decade!'

The entire song was a description of the beauty of the goddess Chandralekha, my character.

In my first and only film down South, I felt privileged that I was one of the first Bollywood female stars Mani had sent a feeler to.

Virtually the whole of 1992, I ended up working on playing *Khalnaika*, the negative but title role, back to back with Chandralekha, the underworld queen of Mani. Two diametrically opposite roles in a year was challenging in more ways than one. Literally fifteen days of each month to either of the two.

With a subtitle 'Revenge her only desire', the intensity and sharply-focused approach of the character in *Khalnaika* was bewitching. Director Sawan Kumar had shown me *The Hand that Rocks the Cradle* and asked if I'd play the lead. When I agreed, he excitedly told his staff: See Anu? An intelligent young girl. Not like our older Bollywood lot! *Phat jaati hai unki 'negative' role ke naam se*...the same old silly romantic girl leads, nothing different they can handle.

The director was proud of me, that always helps the chemistry.

Normally I was not judgmental when I heard of a character. My deciding to do it did not depend on whether she was an angel heart or an evil woman. It was more like—was the character interesting and potent? Did she have the contrasting shades that every real-life character did?

At a movie party at the Taj Hotel in 1993, the legendary Amitabh Bachchan walked up and bent down to my face in superhero gentility, saying:

—Wow! A *Khalnaika*, after just two years of *Aashiqui*!

His appreciation perhaps drew from the fact that I had been nominated for a Filmfare award for *Khalnaika*.

As time went by I was finding it increasingly difficult to respond to the trivial and stupid questions posed by the media. It was not that I minded probing questions on my sexual conduct or a daredevil life; what got my goat was the lack of any homework by most journalists. It tired me.

They were wonderstruck about how a young woman managed life living alone minus parents or a partner. How boring, huh!

The venom of jealousy spread fast in the milk of success. After three years in showbiz, the 'sexy siren' was vomiting blood. The sex goddess who dreamt to be enthroned wanted out.

As a ripe cucumber drops off a vine, I was ready to drop off the Bollywood/modelling cart.

It was a time I was emotionally distressed—my love relationship was in the shadow of gloom.

3

Erotic Experiments

While a movie star, I had relented to TV when I was approached by MTV, which wanted to place its musical foot in India. Based in Hong Kong then, they only had a two-hour slot on Indian television. They wanted to do a flagship show. Looking at the massive appeal Hindi movies had in India, they came up with a new style of presentation—in Hinglish.

As we met at the Oberoi Hotel in Cuffe Parade, they expressed their surprised glee that a top movie star could be interested in becoming a VJ. I told them that I loved their promos, that I could personally relate with them.

Since my days were booked, MTV adjusted time as per my convenience. In a weekly show, I presented a relaxed, conversational style; the tongue-in-cheek impromptu way of VJ-ing was new and creatively sensational. Loved it. And saw what my thigh-high skirt looks like when shot from a low-angle camera.

Tata Tea came around then, asking for an endorsement at a time when Bollywood actors weren't really seen doing that. Brand ambassador was the term being coined—*Anu taazgi de de, Tata ki chai de*...Anu give us freshness, give us Tata tea.

Around the same time an advertising creative head from Lintas nearly prostrated in front of me, begging me to do what he was asking—a condom ad.

I agreed to an unbelievable price for endorsing the condom, in the process propagating the safe art of lovemaking—Kamasutra, here I come.

—O Anu, how could you? You are volunteering to be the brand ambassador for a condom, and that too at the peak of your career? The repercussion would be negative, warned a media mogul.

I did not tell him what I felt—that what the majority in India needs is to break the shackles of repression. That is what geared me right from start. A condom ad was a step forward in the same direction. Even if I was the only model/star to dare to do this.

I recalled Lady Hardinge Hospital, where I had seen desperate women, between the age group of fourteen to forty, stand in a never-ending queue for abortions. Like chickens huddled close together in a slaughter cart, they waited to rid themselves of unwanted, undesirable, illegitimate pregnancy. Some women found the load too much and broke down, either wailed in despair or started to get epileptic fits from a situation they could not escape. As part of the fieldwork for my master's in social work, I had been appointed to counsel such women.

Now, a few years later, my delight was unmatched when as a star I was asked to be the brand ambassador for a condom. I was shouting from the rooftop of fame, to rid people of sexual inhibition, and help save them from getting a child in the womb instead of having to kill it.

Later, I was informed by an ad filmmaker that the 'Pepsi' guys would have considered me for their commercial had it not been for the condom ad...Since when have a soft drink and a condom become competitive products?

In the heady, intolerable mix of an exposed personal life and a public life of fledgling glamour—my work was my saviour. The sea from my Worli apartment rocked, always well-natured, a bit mysterious. Many full moons passed as I lay on the *chattai* of my bare apartment, and moonbathed, alone. Named a style icon by the media in 1994, 'Anusual' was the inventive epithet the journalist Suma Varghese gave me.

The super success of *Aashiqui* had set the ball rolling. I could be pricey and choose to play the lead in one film out of the hundred offered in the glamour cart. I did not have to lick anyone's shoelaces ever, for anything. I had supersuccess. Supersex. Superfame. Superframe. It offered me every candy there was in this world that could lure one. Thank you.

The entertainment news pedlars suspected there was not one, but scores of secret lovers who made me run the impeccable show. And then, as though men were not enough, they were jumping to women. I was outraged at this pre-supposition—I love women as much as I love the truth but I am yet to meet a woman who would stir the sexual drive in me. But where do you start to explain this?

Just then came *Erotica*. A year earlier, a German production house, Regina Zeigler, had had a brainwave— to make an avant garde trilogy under the title *Erotica*. Twelve directors from twelve counties were approached and given a free hand in the depiction of what 'erotic' meant to them. Out of these only three would be finally chosen which would be then financed, the package to open at the Cannes film festival. Mani Kaul, the director chosen from India, asked me to play the lead of an Indian princess, who talks to a parrot about her erotic desires. I could not say no to a film of that high a calibre. I wouldn't just walk the red carpet of Cannes film festival as many stars do, I would have my film opening at international film festivals, on screen for all to watch. Unreal!

CHANDRAMAHAL—PALACE OF THE MOON, NEEMRANA, FEBRUARY 1995

Anything may take place at any time 'cause love does not care for time or order', believed Vatsayana, who penned the *Kamasutra*.

In the pomp and grandeur of an ancient Indian fortress, Kurangi lay alone. Under the full moon, her body glistened with perspiration that came from desire. This was her night. Her erotic lover to-be was finally here.

Her naked high breasts rose and fell with her sensual, heavy breathing. The round depression in her visible navel rose and fell like the waves in the sea do in high tide. The sleek gold waistband on her smooth waist got tilted to the side. The red silk wraparound skirt shone in the finest Rajasthan craftsmanship.

She tingled in anticipation of things to come as she felt the caress of the fine teak floor against her bare shoulders and back. Bathed in moonlight, she could hear the creaking of the wood, the lapping of the water in the lake outside, the peacock performing a rain dance in an effort to attract his mate. Her eyes closed, lips tenderly parted...the ever-abundant shining star of Dhruv shone the brightest ever.

This was her night, her place, her plight.

Here, in Chandramahal, soon will be satiated all her erotic, sexual, sensual fantasies. Her tall, tawny body trembled in expectation of the male touch. The fortress of the moon glistened in an unfulfilled longing.

You will be the first man to make love to me, she thought, as she saw Agrasen stand by her side. She did not voice the words for fear that they might make him hesitate or hold back.

He had entered the large room without her knowing it. The door had been left ajar, for him? He watched the heaviness of the naked breasts of the princess. Just perfect, he thought, the perfect size, neither like little lemons nor large as melon.

Kiss those red luscious lips. Press my chest against those rounded breasts, scratch her with nails Kamasutra-style...He stopped there and pondered—

This wasn't just desire. It felt deeper. It was almost elemental.

With a closer look of the firm nipples, the colour of raw tamarind pulp, he felt an arousal. Her legs almost longer than his, half covered by a red silk garment, showed an eagerness to part. He lowered his head to her face. Their faces came closer as a thousand words remained unsaid, their eyes locked. He pushed his bare chest closer to her, his face went closer to her lips, and lo! the hard thud he heard held him back with restraint, he looked down—it was the same parrot who had carried the invitation of the princess across the river and dropped it from his beak at Agrasen's feet.

'Don't leave me out guys,' shone in the brilliant, bright colours of the parrot. Anu let out a guttural laugh.

He had never seen a woman quite like her.

A goddess, thought he, let me adorn her. He moved down to her feet. On his right, from a large window, twinkled innumerable stars in a miraculously black sky.

Picking a colour made from fresh saffron leaves, he began to paint her toenails...

One evening after shooting I was walking back to my room in Neemrana. Under the luminance of a million stars on the open balcony, I wondered,

—What is the difference between the erotic and pornography?

One teases by showing a bit, by concealing, and the other aims at revealing with a vengeance. Let it all hang out. I prefer the erotic. Sensuality in sexuality. Not just sexuality in sexuality.

In the Neemrana fort sensuality exists in bathing, in acting, in eating, walking, sleeping. Explore your own sensuality.

Each evening shoot begins at 10.30 p.m. and goes on till 6 a.m. One has a feeling of being complete within oneself and, of course, there is a discovery within. Mani Kaul is shooting on a 1.85 format, which is almost like cinemascope, widened and elongated! I'd like to see the results of this.

Mani Kaul paid me a compliment—'I'm amazed to see that dialogue by an actor is not getting in the way of my movement. Normally it is s-o-o-o difficult.' He also likes the fact that I show restraint in revealing the felt emotion.

20 OCTOBER 1995, 6.45 A.M., JAIPUR

Shooting ends. First print will be out in the first or second week of January. Called *Cloud Door*, the film is being processed by Rank Studios, London.

Critic Todd McCarthy raves about *Cloud Door* in *Variety*, the Bible of the Hollywood trade. Calling it a 'stunner in the bunch' of other films chosen by the film festival in Cannes, the critic notes, 'Its pictorial beauty, slow budding sensuality and surprising humour combine to make for a rich effort.'

The New York Times, under a headline, 'Far from Commercial and Quirky to the Hilt', says: '*Cloud Door* becomes a succession of brightly-coloured images that almost tell a story: a beautiful woman, perhaps a courtesan; a green, long-tailed parrot who repeats the erotic phrases he's picked up in her room, potential lovers; a fish that laughs.'

'Anu's Erotic Tale' gets big coverage in *Filmfare*. *Cloud Door* has already been to thirty major film festivals all over the world, and there is a massive article in *Sunday Times*!

Erotica ended up being good in more ways than one; for me it ticked all the boxes: acting, achievement, and glamour. It worked as the final push off the glam-cart I was on. I then took a break from acting, not knowing that I would not be back for a long time.

I could not deny the appreciation from fans had been humbling, but without a personal life left anymore I became restless in Bombay. And when I shared my decision to take a break with Khalid Mohamed, the editor of a leading cine magazine, so I could share it with the public, he refused to print it. And looked at me like I had just bumped my head badly on the topmost rung in the ladder of success.

'No, Anu, you are not leaving. This is unheard of.'

Instead, he started to give the 'young' me a lecture on why I should not have these ridiculous thoughts.

Nobody understood me. It was an emotional whack, it began to assume gigantic proportions—I knew, to keep my sanity, I had to break away from the glambiz.

THEN IN JULY CAME OLIVER: The headline in the paper reported 'Romancing the Stone'; there was a picture of Oliver Stone (an old one) with the caption, 'Stone...smitten.' The article, covering a dinner, stated how Oliver was smitten by Anu Aggarwal, and 'kept moving Anu-wards'.

When Oliver arrived in India, he was stunned—by the kind of appreciation he received from film folks, the few invited to meet him.

On noticing me, he shot towards me like an arrow—an instant association was established between us.

His eyes were still wet from tears after seeing the orphaned, disabled kids in Mother Teresa's home. He confessed his desire to bring his son to India...take him to Varanasi.

And his sharp slated eyes looked enamoured—over dinner—as I hit the dance floor—and when, at 2 a.m., I got exhausted trying hard to avoid the adamant camera glare and walked out in an exasperated frenzy, Oliver followed.

In the garden vista Oliver held my hand tenderly, and admired the gladiola garland on my belly, one that he had sprung across my neck. And exclaimed in disbelief—

'Wow you're Indian? An Indian woman? How come in all that I see around, nobody is like you? You truly are East meets West.'

When parting, he softly whispered, 'Think of this as a dream' and he kissed my cheek, cupping my face gently like I was the most precious thing.

'Come to L.A.'—

Kiss him? No, I did not. Instead, I walked off smouldering. Bursts of a tulip in my heart.

Stifled by the misrepresentations fame brought, I decided to leave, knowing little a popular public persona stays public always. It left people shocked: an actor does not leave when on top. In Bollywood or in Hollywood.

I questioned my decision, Is it rash? Do I really need to leave? Have I really lost it?

But in meditative moments the message was clear—

get away from an unfulfilling, fake existence. Find the Real.

I bought myself a round-the-world J class ticket, went on holiday in style...

Reached Los Angeles, where, after Oliver's birthday dinner, I was driven back to Rick's friend Sanjay's house. Sanjay, who had studied at the Guitar Institute of Technology and who used to be in Rick's band, was now the lead guitarist in a funky hip-hop band in Los Angeles. Sanjay was nursing wounds left by his girlfriend, the beautiful Kajol, who had failed to join him in LA.

Mid-morning, I have just finished meditating in Sanjay's house when the phone rings:

'We are calling from International Creative Management—ICM, one of the leading celebrity management companies in the world. We would like to meet you. Could you please come to Constellation Boulevard for a meeting this afternoon? At two?'

They show a surprisingly keen interest. Hollywood calling!

I arrive at their office in a long black crepe-dress slit to upper thigh, and four-inch high heels; a '70s faded black leather jacket with clasp buttons I picked up from a store in Santa Monica is flung over the dress. I sit opposite the number three in the agency, an Englishman.

'What can you give me that my country has not already?' I smile matter-of-factly.

An interesting hour-long meeting ends with me non-committal, 'I will give it a thought. I fly to New York tonight.'

'Oh! So get in touch with our office in New York then.'

The sun is setting in the leafy courtyard in Sanjay's house. It turns out that Sanjay is also a great cook. Black pepper vodka. Am I signing up with ICM? They promise I will act in only A-grade Hollywood flicks?

As I ponder, comes an answer: Regardless of how good, how A-grade, how much of a money-scorer, a career in Hollywood is not to be pursued; it gives you a lot more of the same that you are bent upon leaving. It may provide more recognition, money in dollars instead of rupees, but it gives you nothing new.

No—Thing that quenches your thirst.

In Mumbai, January of 1996, I receive a call—

—Anuuu, what are you doing this evening?

Mukund Mausaji's soothing voice on phone gets me thinking. An appropriate reply would be, 'Nothing,' and I love it. Last year I had bought a round-the-world ticket for myself. Disappeared from Bollywood, modelling, even endorsements. Had I really lost it? People around me thought I had.

I had been busy guarding my new-found privacy. Before I could consciously frame an answer, Mukund Mausaji said with zest,

'Nothing, I am sure, now that you are not doing films/modelling...why don't you come this evening to Sir JJ School of Arts? For a talk on yoga? Do you want me to pick you up? 6 p.m.?'

At the school, with my eyes and sunburnt golden brown face under cover, I heard the phantasmal figure on stage give the most phenomenal talk I had ever heard. For an hour I paid rapt attention to the gentle male voice:

There is a body, and there resides consciousness about our interactions with the world—the conscious sheath. Inside the body is the mind; emotions, feelings, and impressions reside here. And inside that is the soul or the supreme, the actual seat of our 'real' self—our seed, the centre. In a normal human being all three, the body, the mind, and the soul, are disconnected. We are unbalanced. We are far from the centre. And we don't know that. Yoga can help find the harmony among the three. Get the head, heart, and hand to work in cooperation. Coalition. Alignment. Cohesion. Harmony.

That's cool, I thought. I don't want to continue living threadbare. I felt sure, too, that if all three forces united in me, then I would be one with the ultimate. In that instance I knew that acting even in Hollywood would only make me an international star, but if yoga gives what it promises then I would be a universal being. International versus Universal. The choice was simple—Universal.

Towards the end of his 'What is Yoga' talk, the guru made all of us close our eyes and guided us to a Chakra meditation. In those twelve minutes, as I rotated my consciousness from the base of the spinal cord—the

Mooladhara Chakra—all the way up to the crown of the head—the Sahasrara Chakra—I had an uncanny experience. From the stage in front a blob of light came hurtling towards me and entered the forehead. This luminosity then expanded and kept growing till my entire body was filled with the fluorescence of light.

Feeling a bit 'copulated' from that occurrence, I managed to shakily get up. A person walked up to me and gave me an application form for the yoga university the superyogi had talked about...and I applied as a student.

Let us go back to the roots.

Yoga, here I come.

The MLA from Aurangabad, Maharashtra, Sri Peshavrao Antaile, landlord of my Worli flat, looked a typical politician-type, what with his Gandhi *topi*, folded white *dhoti*, and Nehru jacket.

He spouted Gandhian philosophy but under his cap lay deceit. What with a paltry government income, his main aim was to squeeze me dry. I was naïve, and overworked. Shooting three shifts a day, I considered it a matter of pride that I made it to the set on time. Antaile would regularly appear at my door with his slimy laughter. One early morning, just as I had finished my first cup of coffee, he showed up: 'Anu, I need five lakh rupees. *Kya karein, bahut buri haalat hai.*'

I did not know that he was not just greedy, he was

covered with slime of the worst sort. He was chirping like a grasshopper, jumping between the building society and me, singing the tune of the poor sufferer. It was a bolt out of the blue when one day I received a call from the society with which I had not had much contact with till then. To cut a long story short, he had told the society a putrid lie—that I was not paying the rent, that I was a terrible tenant, and that they should help him in evacuating me from the flat.

I was flabbergasted by the betrayal—how could he? When I called him he was unwilling to talk, bossed me around like he was the loaner and I the borrower of Rs 5 lakhs, a big sum in 1993.

That year, Rick was not the only one who stabbed me in the back. There were others who went out of the way to do so.

With no family around, meditation was my saviour—this too shall pass, I thought. And look: sorrow and happiness exist together. Your palpable success has to get balanced with knife stabs in the back. Do what you can. With a calm mind you can do the best you can. Stay cool, and collected. Yes.

And it so happened that the vey next day the owner of Pet Airline, a big fan, dropped in to see me, with a friend. 'Meet my friend Mr Gagrat, the owner of the top law firm Gagrat & Co in Mumbai,' he said proudly.

Wow. That was just what I needed, a lawyer. Astonished at the way help had just brushed the creepers hanging on the gate, and was paying me a visit, I thanked the million stars in the universe.

Gagrat introduced me to Gagrat & Co., and they instantly, and with great urgency, began to study the case. It turned out that the total amount I had paid in spurts over a period of three years, was enough for buying two flats.

I stared in disbelief at Gagrat, I was tongue-tied.

Antaile was on the run now. Gagrat managed to trace him, scare him, and hook him.

We filed a lawsuit to get a 'resident' status.

Politicians are not supposed to nick the common folk; Gagrat & Co put fear in Antaile. Now it was his turn to call me. The raging lion had become a meek mouse.

Next we won the 'resident ownership'.

Then in 1997 it became legal for the politicians like Antaile to sell property they had bought for a pittance, through a lottery pick in chit funds. I had waited to buy the flat from him. And Antaile, of course, without a trace of shame, started to plead for some more money than the selling cost of the flat. On my way to yogashram I was not in the mood for a delay. We paid him whatever extra he wanted. The building society was almost apologetic now. Take your time, they said. I was relaxed. I saw this as jumping through another hoop to win my way to yoga.

4

Falling in Love...with Yoga

Sex isn't a need. At best it is a seasonal desire.

I was thinking last night what it'd be like if I shaved off all the hair from my head and joined a Buddhist nun-monk order. And then never again craved a hamburger or Camembert souffle or sex or Mysore masala dosa or get millions in cash for being a glam puss.

LET GO. Attachment creates fear. Fear leads to clinging. Clinging leads to more fear. More fear lays out destruction.

At a time when some fans wondered about and lamented the disappearance of Anu Aggarwal, what they did not know was that in the Himalayan terrain I wilfully lay on flowerbeds and counted the shooting stars. Under a powder-black sky. Zero noise. Zero pollution. Zero disturbances from unwanted male attention or the prying media. There is a scene in *Aashiqui* where my lover helps me escape the orphanage from a tyrant patron who perhaps had a sadomasochistic kind of attraction towards the character I play. We run away. We run till the edge of a mountain. Panting and a bit shaky, I view the magnificence of nature, just hills and the sky, and ask my lover boy with bated breath,

'Is this heaven? *Kya ye swarg hai?*'

'Yes, Anu, this is heaven.'

And he pulls my breathless mouth towards his for a kiss...

Now in the yogashram, lying under the translucent sky, alone, breathing naturally and rhythmically, it was unrelentingly clear—yes, this was 'heaven'. I was in it.

The first time he—Swamiglee, whose discourse I had heard in Mumbai—saw her passport-sized picture in the application form, he was captivated by her beauty, and knew it was not just physical. The denim collar was invitingly stretched over a delicate neck. The pointed corner of the collar touched a determined jaw. Her bright deer's eyes leapt out of the white sheet of paper. Secret scents unfolded in the striking image. Behind her friendly smile he saw a simple, hard-working girl, with immense good karma. No wonder then the master of discrimination had found it hard to get his eyes off the picture.

In the questionnaire, when asked about my

profession, I'd written 'student'. It was a moment when my status as a movie icon weighed heavily on me. My admission should not be based on my being a star. Let merit be the deciding factor. No favours granted. Play the role of a student again, in real life, with full power. Become a Nobody again—a learner.

Of late I had been tiring of hearing my own voice saying the same things. I knew I needed time out. It was October 1993. I had shot my last cover for *Cine Blitz* magazine, which ran a five-page interview in which I was asked:

—Anu, do you like women?

I did not dodge the question, or get offended. I smiled wryly and said,

—Of course, I love women. My first love was a woman—my mother.

I stated a fact.

Well, generally, I liked people. Sexually? I preferred men. Why? They had something that we women didn't have. The male anatomy, to begin with. It was that simple.

And I always wondered where that prying question came from. Media fabrication?

The media liked her. It was a surprise to them that after just three successful rollicking years in the business of glamour she would disappear.

Soon I received a letter from the yogashram stating my application had been chosen. I was called to Degirivan, Uttarakhand, a region of outstanding beauty.

On 30 September 1997, under a clear sky, a palatial, massive campus greeted me, in quietude, and I entered the large metal gate of the fort of knowledge.

Then the first round of scrutiny—we had to pass a written examination. I found it impressive that my college grades, which boasted excellence in sociology/anthropology, were not enough for admission.

The few chosen ones were then called for a personal interview.

'Why yoga? Why do you want to learn...Why?'

The skinny teacher/interviewer, a yogi, wore a puzzled look—in his long red robe and bare skull. Star-model Anu? Wants to live in a village in remote serenity and learn the discipline of yoga?

'I have read an ordinary human being uses only 2 per cent out of 10 of his brain's total potentiality. I want to use all 10. I suspect yoga can show me how,' I replied with the utmost earnestness; I did not blink.

The admission list on the board showed names of forty-five students, out of hundreds, who had been selected. Out of an array of eager students from twenty-odd countries.

Anu Aggarwal was the second name on the list of those chosen.

My first night at the yogashram I was given a room that really surprised me—in a yoga university I would not have imagined cobwebs hanging in clusters all around the walls and on the ceiling. Immediately, I was looking around the building for a broom and duster.

'This room had been lying locked up. Guruji instructed you be given this room.'

The stiff-lipped swami in-charge of women's quarters showed an uneasy disdain.

'Cleaning material will be available in the morning. At 6 a.m. We are particular about timings here,' the Polish swami had hair loss of the kind that happens to cancer patients after chemotherapy.

'Besides, it is 7 p.m. and it is *mouna* time, we will observe being quiet, no verbal dialogue till 7 a.m. 7 to 7 is *mouna*, didn't you read that in the discipline schedule on the board near the reception?' I did a swift about-turn and walked off. Wow! That was sticky. So then Swamibitteryogi ought to have had the room cleaned before she gave it? Pray, tell, how does she expect me to sleep in a webzine of spiders? Yoga should teach some basic cleanliness? Here I was, out to help. I had asked for cleaning material, in a polite city way. But the swami was amazingly impolite, like I had invaded her private space or something. Due to this obtrusive start I had to sleep out in the open under the magnanimous stars, but it was not that unpleasant a night.

It was like going back in time. The rawness of the place had an almost uncomfortable simplicity—toilet rolls, for instance, were nowhere to be seen. And then the fakeness of superiority sported by the sanyasi lot was off-putting.

Our yoga course manager, an American, was rumoured to hide leftover chocolate slabs under her mattress. Since sanyasis were not supposed to miss what they were not given, life must be tough. We called her Charlie Chocolatoga—she with her pear-shaped body and a smile that always looked like it was a massive effort.

The non-Indianness of our teachers showed not just in their white hairless heads, but in how they mispronounced Hindi and Sanskrit words in theory classes...

Having been born in an open-minded family rooted in deep spiritual tradition, I had been brought up with my paternal grandmother reciting the Srimad Bhagwad Gita—these were my bedtime stories. My maternal grandfather woke up each morning with a smile, chanting Kr'sna with deep reverence. My grandfather introduced me to *Autobiography of a Yogi* by Swami Yogananda when I was six, and I found myself in awe of Babaji, the forever living saint.

Suddenly I was finding a lost beginning of my own heritage...I felt more Indian than ever.

After dinner at 5 p.m., when we were still in the last few throes of an exuberant October sun, we would have the evening programme. No doubt this was a stunning setting: the trees, the squirrels, the exotic fruits of the forest, and the waters of the Ganga. And I walked around mesmerized, in silence, in the fifteen minutes between dinner and *keertan*, my loose muslin garment billowing away from the body. Naked spirituality.

Between 6 p.m. and 7 p.m. we quietly heard the swamis, who were new to the Hindu gods, play the harmonium and sing devotional songs. The mispronunciation of the gods' names—Rrrrraammma, Keeshnaaa—were like drops of poison in my ears, and I wanted to go home.

I wondered how the patron had just those four teachers do everything—from teaching to singing—and we saw them during meal times in the kitchen, too. So if a teacher did not like you, there was no way you could get away from them, or they from you.

The food supplied there left an awful lot to be desired. In the name of *saatvik* food we were given black tea with lots of sugar for breakfast at 6.30 a.m. Lunch at 11 a.m. was dal and either potato or beans they grew locally. Dinner at 5 p.m. was again potato curry, and if you managed to reach early and jump the queue then you would be lucky to get a piece of bread.

My diet since school days and then while modelling—has been of crucial importance. The foodie and the creative cook in me doted on cheese and yoghurt. Take that calcium, Ma would always say. The grapevine in the ashram was that many years ago, an Australian sanyasi had gotten sick and vomited blood after drinking tea with milk. I hear it was Swamiglee's guru, Bade Swamiglee, who banned not only milk but its products as well from entering the yogashram.

And then, of course, the fact that they did not believe in salads was pretty shocking.

I could have ignored food, shelter, clothing, and even the sanyasi lot, had I got hooked on to the course I had so earnestly looked forward to. But the quality of the teachers spoilt it. I felt personal disappointment regarding the structure of the yoga course—I found the classes boring and I had my bags packed in less than ten days.

I was ready to leave. The patron, Swamiglee, was puzzled (he had never come across such a case before, I was supposed to be one of the privileged forty-five students from twenty different countries selected. Besides, not even a leaf fluttered without his permission.)

'Why...?' he asked. He had his gaze fixed on me. He looked calm, steady and relaxed.

And I told Swamiglee with an air of confidence, 'I've got better things to do.'

I looked away into the Ganga behind his erect yogic back, for it was the Ganga I was going to miss. I was reminded of how, just eight months ago, Harvey, my second boyfriend of Jewish descent (after the Giorgio Armani model Danielle) had taken a picture of me in Australia's Frazer Island—my back to the camera, in my black swimsuit, walking into the river, the water level till my upper thigh. Deep-sea diving in the Great Barrier Reef was one of my last worldly encounters before getting here.

'Why do you want to leave something unfinished?

You came here to learn about yoga, you ought to complete the course, get the certificate, then go. Leaving is never the answer.'

He made a brusque turn towards his office; his movements signified the chapter was closed.

On that windy October day, I had agreed partly to what he had just said. Another couple of months is no big deal, I argued to myself—I stayed.

From then on I was taken under his long and stretchable yogi wings. A special and undivided attention by the head of the university followed after that. Under the laps of the glorious moon he looked after me. He understood my needs: he warded off any prying media, and protected me from unwanted male attention.

And, of course, I would discover he did not want me to leave even after we finished the course...

I fell in love with yoga.

5

A Smitten Swami

The breeze a lot cooler, some new flowers opening up their shoots, it was the start of November, and the paddy fields in the distance looked lush. I found I was acclimatizing to the quaint and quiet serenity of the yogashram. One day I was walking along admiring the quiet beauty of the campus when I was stopped. The tall yogi stood right in front of me. I hadn't heard the hiss of his wooden sandals or even a soft pant of breath. Living silence. His stark gaze, beyond a silent admiration for the body, penetrated my being. I was receptive; I allowed it.

'What all do you know?'

His face hardly ever changed the benign expression.

The empty, abundant fields of the yogashram seemed the only witness.

'I know now how little I do.'

I caught his quiet appreciation of me. I saw him take a quick look at the straight auburn hair on my waist dancing in Ganga breeze. I gently smiled.

—Will you have tea with me this afternoon? Come to my office at tea break.

The passive softness in his clear voice, carried the promise of a new beginning.

His invitation for tea was said to be a rarity, almost unheard of.

—Sure.

My answer conveyed my surprise.

His bare head is larger than his slim body. A firm yogi neck. I sense his virgin sexuality.

An hour later, I get a flyer.

Black letters printed on a recycled white sheet—they recycled everything, a totally biodegradable way of existence, a return to nature. We studied about the elements—water, fire, air—and how their composition formed us; we re-established the forgotten connect we have with nature. We learnt the art of living and experienced the strict discipline of living it.

—Come for TEA!!!!

Funny—his excitement. But getting unadulterated attention without calling for it was something I had first learnt to accept just before I started menstruation, as a teenager.

I am a student again—my new and exciting reality. Breathtaking setting. Soon the distance expanded: between me and the money-spinning machine I had been. I was not managing money anymore, or keeping abreast of the finance market to invest. I chose to be out of public display. I thanked the heavens with all the fervour of a new convert. What an incredible joy that was! In the purity of yoga and no real personal goals of either achievement or success, I had truly entered a state of non-materialism. With zero pollution and the silence of the Ganga, I almost could not believe how happy I was. I could not expect any more from life.

He watches her with keen intensity. Intently. He has never seen anyone like her. She has a bag full of surprises. For instance, when he asked her if she would take a guru mantra and a spiritual name (normally disciples begged, pleaded, asked him for the same) she was forthright:

—My guru resides within me. Even though I do not follow his advice all the time, I am in touch with him.

That was that.

Over a period of time it seemed he had come to adore her. He cherished each day as he saw her walk around the picturesque campus, her spine erect and gait absolutely straight in loose, flowing attire, the light fawn skin glowing.

One day in his *satsang* he cracked a joke, with a straight face, and heard a loud bellow of laughter. She was the only one who laughed. The other 1,200 people sitting around her on the mat were either lost in their mental babble and missed what he had said, or did not catch the humour, or thought it irreverent to laugh in front of the Big Guru. She was smart and she was fearless. He liked that. Good karma.

What delighted him most was: Anu the social innovator was ever involved in Karmayoga, one of the principles of the science of life. She did it even when it was not a part of the strict schedule of the yoga course. Karmayoga, loosely speaking action done while renunciating the fruit of such action, is a thing of distinctive importance: it accrues infinite gains for a Karmayogi. The patron saw gain in placing a Bollywood star, now a Karmayogi, as a model before other yoga aspirants. For most it was hard to believe. Out of the forty-five students in the yoga course, from twenty different countries, with only four Indians, Anu came across as the most hard-working.

Any act performed with sincere gratitude cleanses the mind. When not in the theory class, she was either seen in the kitchen sitting on the floor in front of big vats of dal, cooking vegetables in a curry, serving food to yoga students and sanyasis, or in the garden outside removing weed, or in her coconut grove talking to and hugging the trees and cooing—what she said to them was anybody's guess. Or she was seen helping in baking bread, rolling out wheat *chapattis* on the floor, in her yogi clothing. On Sundays the students took rest from the demanding yoga course, a ruthless week where the classes and the syllabus of the course taught a historical, anatomical, psychological, physical, psychosomatic approach to the discipline of yoga—a humane outlook to self as well as to the other.

When the patron was a little boy-sanyasi his guru had referred to Karmayoga as the be-all of all yoga. The action, when performed without expectation of a reward, or even a sense of achievement, is the highest of all different kinds of yoga. A society which has in its midst such Karmayogis, who have identified themselves with those around them, forgetting their selfish interests, will have prosperity, order and harmony.

It was only a couple of months later I understood what the crux of our yoga course was: in essence we studied how to get back to the Source. Fascinating! A way of thinking, behaving, and finding what actually matters, all that we tend to ignore in city life—an ignorance that comes from a narrow perspective about life. Here, in the yogashram, we were learning how to excel, how to maximize human potential. Marvellous! I had found the reason why I was born on earth. And who I really was. However attractive it might have been, how could even Hollywood have given this to me? I was surer than ever I had made the right choice—even though I had at times felt a prickly regret for not taking up the offer of the International Creative Management agency to sign me up.

But what was interesting was—there was another side

of me that was revealing itself now. A recipient of appreciation from fans, I was now ready to give. Love, this time. Karmayoga, here I come!

Yoga was changing the despondency I had felt, the pitfalls I had faced, it was transforming it to joy. Love life.

Know your body, know yourself.

Bare attention. Still the body. Calm the mind. Become aware of your feelings. Be a witness. Watch. Watch instead of reacting. Drop the terrible, habitual complexes of city dwellers.

Just be. Be you. We, unfortunately, don't learn that in school.

Of the theory we studied, there was only one physical *asana* class. And that was at 4.30 a.m. I followed my one-hour meditation routine, which meant I was in the *asana* hall at 3.30 a.m., sitting on my mat in the dark hush of the leaves in the palm trees outside the hall. I then began—to subdue this monkey mind.

The patron of the yogashram had spiritual fans who slept with his picture under their pillow. During the day they waited endlessly for him to cross their walking path. Loose clothing did not complement his body but it hardly mattered. They were in awe of him. Those lucky times when he did straddle across, stopped and asked them a question or greeted them, they would freeze, get tongue-tied.

What did they see in him? I could never fathom.

He was a bit odd. Stunned at the absurdity of the questions he would ask, in that gorgeous pictorial setting, I would think: What a waste.

The only commonality we nurtured: He was a star, in the spiritual realm, and I just escaped being a star in the material realm. Incognito.

Yoga stipulated that I be a observer and I dutifully took it on. He was the first on my bare-attention watch-list: Disciples bent to touch his feet, his robust Alsatian dog Shambhoo wagging his tail next to him in acknowledgement; the lithe yogi plugged on to four different phone calls responded with extreme yogic ease, guiding the centres in twelve different countries the yogashram had a presence in; speaking fourteen foreign languages with ease, his mellow yogic smile intact. A swami always in glee, Swamiglee.

I wondered: Is this man, born to a parson, ordained in sanyas when four years old, for real?

Then, like a contortionist, he could kiss his toenail, put his naked head between his legs and do the cartwheel in the Himalayan air. Enormous, long and supple legs walked with an alarming lightness. Even when he walked fast his movements were like the ebb and flow of the Ganga, easy and natural. The hero in that spiritual realm sorted out the problems of damsels in distress from around the world. The Phantom who walked.

But I was not in distress, and I did not choose him to be my guardian. Even though he towered over me when we stood, which was new as most Indian men were shorter than me. Even in Bollywood they found it hard to find a hero taller than me. Besides, since childhood I was exposed to a super-fit Pa, who wore the same-size jeans at sixty that he did at eighteen, when he was training to be an engineer in the air force.

With his head a size too big for his narrow shoulders and slim body, the patron was far from the 'perfect man', my Prince Charming. His muscle tone was incredibly low, and his gait had a kind of passive, feminine delicacy. 'Aren't they too big?' he had twisted his ears one day; they did look like the flapping ears of an elephant. He was being funny but it told me I was becoming his friend. He had a complex about his ears, and I felt he had made a kind of a confession; I wanted to tell him:

—Come on Swamiglee, enroll for a ten-day course in Vipassana. Where a deep surgical operation of the mind can uproot the deepest of all complexes.

I didn't for fear he might take it as a rejection, especially in his ode to impress me.

And he continued to keep an eagle eye on me.

A month had flown by faster than the Ganga wave. I was there to have tea with him. Why had he called me, when he didn't anyone else? I was just another student.

That autumn afternoon he sat in a yogic stance on a wooden chair, a laptop on his table. His eyes were glued to the door when I entered his office—like he knew I was there. Was it my flip-flop sandals he heard when I was some distance away?

Awareness.

In the yogi's room, a *yantra* (a flat metal plate with geometrical figures etched on it in triangular pattern), rested like family pictures do in urban homes, and the shaved head of a fragile figure in a rusty gown, the Yoga Nidra teacher, made some gentle movements. What is she doing here? Perhaps she is invited for tea too? Oh no! Look, she is here to serve us. Must be Karmayoga assigned to her. Karmayoga of ultimate surrender.

In yoga, relaxation from tensions is of prime concern; the practice of Yoga Nidra, yogi sleep, does just that. The art of deep relaxation was one of my favourite practices. It would get so deeply embedded in me that I would wake up from coma practising it; less than two years later.

Living with basic everyday necessities, a glass and a plate, fine cutlery did not exist in the yogashram. Or so I thought. It was a delight to have tea in fine rose-embossed porcelain mugs, served on a copper tray. And that too milk tea I hadn't tasted in a month!

His eyes were steady—his gaze fixed on me. I looked into the depth of his eyes and I was astounded: he was not staring at me like fans did or designers taking my size did, but it was as if he had entered inside me. My persona was being ripped apart with the utmost gentility. I allowed him in. Inner peace met inner peace. Got locked. Intertwined like the leaves of two trees which, growing apart, had started to grow into each other. And suddenly I was taken away, far from the freshly mowed lawn outside, the Ganga shimmering in the morning light.

This was ultimate respect and love—he wanted to know me, touch that part in me that is the real me, the bigger part, the innermost inside me, call it God or whatever exists inside each. And when he did, it was a peep into the mystery of life I always looked for but did not know.

Inebriated, I could neither blink nor breathe—I lost the sense of time and space. And knew that this is what I'd been waiting for. I'd been led to the fortress of my deepest desire. Unbelievable, Unreal.

Shuffling a file on his uncluttered desk, he did not look at me as he asked a question, his manner gentle and casual.

'What is the name of your grandfather?'

What??

His idea of conversation one would have over tea left me a bit baffled.

'Khushi Ram Singh. A family tree of fourteen generations has Devi Singh come from Rajasthan to Uttar Pradesh and buy land, lots of it...he is the first grandfather in the lineage.'

I reckoned it was time to leave. I got up.

On seeing me get up before he signalled I should stay. He looked perplexed.

Power wears many different masks but the essence of it is always the same—it pumps up the ego and deflates it when somebody in your surroundings does not respond to it as you see others do.

And a master who runs a yoga university should perhaps grow up.

I walked off fast. And I could feel his concentrated eyes devour my back, perhaps run up and down the straight silver line of the spinal cord?

Why can he not be straight with me? Ask me what he wants instead of dodging.

In 1997, yoga had not caught on with Indians fast enough even though yoga is rooted in the Indian soil. I was the only Indian girl among the priveleged forty-five students.

My room was changed. With the magnanimous Ganga as a backdrop in the large windows, and the sense of serenity and silence it brought, I was now sharing a room with an English girl, Gail. An art student, she came from a village outside London, detested waking up at 4 each morning as the course demanded. In the mornings she would turn on full lights at 3 a.m., and rush around the room frowning, as if she had just had a nightmare. Talking was not allowed. I covered my eyes with the pillow and hoped she would calm down.

So we hardly communicated.

But I admired the fact that she never complained.

The twenty-one-year-old had been assigned the Karmayoga to clean all the six toilets in our House of Shakti. From 7 a.m. to 8 a.m. she would be seen humming to herself as she performed the task. And to take a break she would walk silently into the room, heat some water in the kettle, and have one of the teas she had carried from the UK—Earl Grey or Camomile. The sweet smell lingered in the zero-pollution air. Then, she would casually walk back to the toilets, her blonde brown hair stroking her forehead, and resume the cleaning.

It was so matter-of-fact, unlike the problem we Indians see it to be.

Yoga believes in a holistic approach. Holistic living is the art of maintaining a balance between ourselves and our environment. Understand and respect that we are connected with everything around us.

Each moment was one of learning for me. It was seeping deep inside my being.

On Gail, the changes gradually showed up. We were a quarter of the way through in our yoga course when the dimples appeared, Gail started to smile. The effects of yoga were obvious. We became buddies.

On a festive holiday she did a numerological study on me. The dark brown mole on the white of her face expanded as she huffed, 'It is exactly like that of Dalai Lama! All digits in his chart and yours are the same, except one...'

'Must be that one different digit...arouses the devil...'

But it was a comparison that made me feel like I had just received the biggest compliment in my life.

Gail brushed off my lightness, and insisted,

'Numbers show you have a vast resemblance to the Dalai Lama...your charts are almost the same.'

The marigolds were always in full bloom. I was eager to compliment the manager for the overall beauty and the management of the yogashram, but each time our paths crossed (there was no way we could ignore any sanyasi, we ate together in silence, we slept in the same quarters, we attended the same evening programme), Swamiflusteryogi would pretend to look at a fallen dead leaf in the yogashram. She made sure she avoided any interaction with me.

Small pumpkin breasts on large bulbous hips seemed to carry a tale of neglect, though I could not have guessed what the problem was.

But when she caught me talking to another student, teacher, or Swamiglee, she would hear me with rapt attention. At such time her large ears popped out, inside her shiny sanyasi pate she dismantled me...

In her shaved, egg-shaped head her dislike of Anu was evident, it was anybody's guess why. There was a new set of mysteries the yogashram would unfold. I was pleasantly alarmed to see myself stay unscathed. Almost nothing bothered me anymore. Calmness flew in the breeze.

The simple loose clothing I wore seemed to be a fashion statement of modesty. 'Feeling' overtook 'showing'. Feel it, rather than show it. Clothes included. The silence of each day surrendered to the start of the next. Months passed. I tried hard to check the fast pace and scattered movements of the normal mind in each act we performed. In rolling out dough, in acute silence, I practised to live in the present moment.

Little did I know that on the other side of my serene fairytale existence in the yogashram, brewed a plot to disturb that very fibre.

It was the warm month of April. So far, Swamiflusteryogi had stood quietly in the background, without a whimper, and seen the patron's fondness for Anu grow.

In the yogashram the gates for any class were closed ten minutes before the class began.

And if you were marked absent in two classes you would be told to go home, as happened to a Spanish yoga student. I liked that strict regimen; not because I liked to be on time, but it told me we were in good hands so far as the seriousness of the yoga course went.

Yoga is not confined to a country. We talk of cosmic vibes. We uproot things intangible to the common eye. Like in class today at 9.30 a.m., we were being told about the five winds, the *vayus*, that exist in the human body, and the five separate directions they move in. The physical structure of the body hides the winds like a secret that man himself forgot. In all human physical structures the hardware is identical, only the software changes.

The students had the freedom to choose their seats in the class. Each day was a different seat. That day I chose a chair next to the window. With paddy fields in the distance the mud on the banks of the Ganga looked crystallized. Molecules of abundance in each grain of sand, I was delighted with the cosmic beauty outside. The breathtaking quietude was overwhelming.

Suddenly, an apparition appeared. I was alarmed to see the still image move, however slightly, and break into a benign smile. Ah! Swamiglee, what is he doing here?

He was standing behind two trees in such a way that only I could see him. I fathomed he had come to see me. And his image became bigger, like I was zooming into him. This was all a bit strange, and I could not help but be slightly amused and pleased as well. I heard him, without him speaking. Can he just leave me alone? Flattered as I was, this was like being under some strict vigilance—he followed me at *keertan* time, now he reminded me of my school days where a classmate, Ashish, played pranks with me. But I did like that relaxed stillness in his body and the simplicity in the smiling face.

6

A Levitating Superyogi

After the class I am called to his office. Now what?

I walk into his office, the Ganga behind shimmers in dubious secrecy.

The patron, long-lashed, sits in yogic lightness behind an empty desk, a laptop the only object between us. He is focused on me.

—I have your picture in my room.

A vast smile reveals a perfectly healthy set of light pink gums.

What?? Got my picture in his room? A fan?

Worldly people—fans—have pictures of stars, and spiritual seekers frame pictures of their gurus and wear them in a pendant or hang them at a special place on the wall. My photo?

Discovery: Gurus have pictures of a chosen goddess of supreme wisdom, the *Mahavidyas*. Worship of the female devis was perhaps a part of Tantra.

—I want to dress up for you. This evening...I will show you Devi Goddess Matangi...You look exactly like her...Will you come?

I like his no-nonsense approach: he comes straight to the point. No social formalities, not even a 'How are you?'

The squirrel on the broad trunk of the tree behind him scurries up in a hurry, cautiously, a glance back every few steps just to see if a predator followed...

What did he just say?

Be aware of the responses your body has: my heart had missed a beat, breath locked for that minuscule of a second, doves of adulation cooed, in the total silence within me.

Me, a goddess?

I am sinfulness personified. I am a cynic. A sceptic. From a diva to devi?

Why is he saying this?

He had just elevated me from being a city belle, a movie star, to a cosmic entity whom the gurus worshipped. Astral worldly existence. Wow!

'Matangi, the only dark smoke-skinned goddess, amongst the nine fair others, is one of the ten *Mahavidyas*...'

Is this a part of my inner truth I am here to learn? In the plush, lascivious setting this was to be a dream come true. A dream I never knew was a dream.

—Come to my *kutir* this evening, I will show you.

His haven at 6 p.m., I step into the cool quietude of his enormous garden. A conch is placed on the side of the door, laminated and illuminated by moonlight. The door is open.

A sensational dark descends, my face bends towards the flames of innumerable candles lit alongside the path. The entire passageway, next to the rose bushes, holds a pure magical hue. I am on way to the open door. Openness is a rare but enduring quality.

In the pitch darkness of a village sky, without a touch of bright streetlights, a rare beauty is ignited. A sweet smell lingers in the thin air.

Earlier that evening I sat on my bed. Thoughtlessly. Watched the Ganga glint from my window. Basking in the serenity of the place, I was intimidated. If there is one thing I am a fan of, it is the Ganga. Gail, in a loose long white dress, walked in carrying a bunch of exotic white flowers.

—Aren't they stunning?

—Love your hair, Anu! It is like pure silk. Can I weave these in your hair?

—Sure, I say.

Sword-shaped white petals stick out of my head. I wore a white crocheted blouse with spaghetti strings from Aurobindo ashram, Pondicherry. White spandex leggings from a modelling job in New York City. A semi-transparent muslin *dhoti* with gold edges, bought in Chennai when shooting with ace director Mani Ratnam, was the six-yard fabric wrapped on my legs.

Wear the dress, forget the dress: a model's display ideology. Just walk. Pine straight and tall.

I was walking into the woods, in a storyteller's dream, when a clear recognizable male voice stopped me.

—Let me make you a drink...champagne?

Champagne? Really? In a yogashram?

Suddenly, my silenced head jangled. The man-made habitations I left behind are silenced, and now champagne in this serenity.

The large living room, mostly bare, was scented with a fresh fragrance of cleanliness. There were some symbolic *yantras* in an open cane bookshelf, a Sony amplifier, two low red sofas with raw cotton covers and no cushions (Swamiglee had made me sit on one), and a tiny, square hollow pit on the floor that was the *havan kund*.

In his haven, a rectangular modern hut in a large garden, Swamiglee spent his time alone. With unbreakable enthusiasm and unquestioned discipline, he practised his *sadhana*. Here he performed a *havan* where he worshipped fire in coal and wood, as he sprinkled aromatic incense ridden herbs in it. This was his way to link with positive, cosmic energy. Or he focused on a *yantra* placed in front of him. He mediated the positive vibes to the world.

Swamiglee returned, delicately handing me a steel glass. Never much of a drinker, I was curious to know if it really was champagne, and took an instant small sip. *Ahh.* But, of course, it was pure distilled water. With a mischievous glint in his sharp eyes, Swamiglee watched me with rapt yogic attention. Subliminal intensity. His gaze dazed me.

I understood: pure water is the best champagne in the world.

After I finished the 'champagne', we stepped out into the garden. The light of the candles was gently ablaze alongside the length of the garden.

'You are nothing like thousands of people I have seen.'

By this he meant his devotees, yoga aspirants, and followers worldwide. He barely spoke, and when he did each letter was a sparkling gem pearl...

I stayed quiet. In the pin-drop silence of the place I heard a squirrel move.

—You have an open mind...a vastness, he said, as if he were speaking the truth of the Vedas.

I turned my neck to see crackles of profuse light bursting. Around the pathway all buds of the planted roses seemed to spring open.

I was astonished.

I looked back to where he was standing, but he was not there.

I looked around for him in the darkness of the still beauty of the garden.

There he was—at the other end of the large garden. Before I could ask how he moved so fast and reached the other end of the place something seemed odd—his body was raised from the ground—he was flying in the air! His happy face under a bald pate had a magnificent aura.

Gosh! He is flying? I had first learnt about levitation when I studied Maharishi Mahesh Yogi's tract on transcendental meditation. He believed that if a collective group of meditators levitated together it would create a dynamic change in the wellness of humans. And in one of the retreats I attended in Triyambakeshwar in Maharashtra, one of the meditators started to levitate when we meditated. He had hopped like a tadpole with his eyes closed. With the strange sound I heard in the hush of the place, I had peeked sideways, and wondered about the safety of other meditators who sat with eyes shut—he could hit someone, the frog. Then, I was amazed—he was abnormally conscious of others' presence around him as he hopped in one straight line, his pace and rhythm unaltered. Transcendental flying!

But Swamiglee levitates with his eyes open and while standing? The one difference was he was also smiling in a benevolent fashion!

I must be dreaming...how did he appear on the opposite side of the garden? How did he get an aura? But before I could dwell on the physicality of it all, a sudden burst of high energy and joy exploded inside me, and simultaneously he appeared right in front of me, where he was standing originally. And as he bent down to pat his Alsatian dog Shambhoo, I realized his body was incredibly flexible. He raised his head and smiled innocently at my shocked reaction.

A bit mystified by the mystic being, I felt a bit enamoured.

—I have your picture in my room!

He had asked I come along to his haven to see the picture of the goddess of smoke, Matangi. He had insisted I looked exactly like her, but as I walked back to my room in the House of Shakti, it struck me—he was revealing what was inside him. Exposing his transcendental qualities and mine that lay hidden in me. Awaken your goddess qualities—you are not just a mortal. The intensity of the encounter left me breathless with adoration. And the stars shone on us brilliantly well.

The woman in me was waking up, I crocheted small pouches for the sanyasis, I made booties for the village children. I stitched the patron a fashionable scarf (apart from the red robe his clothes left much to be desired).

It certainly makes me feel special, but why does he keep following me, the superyogi? Privileges always brought responsibility.

—Anu! where were you? I was expecting to see you on stage, Swamiglee had halted me once again, in the lawn outside the hall, where a function was taking place.

It was Christmas of 1997. The students sang hymns,

performed skits. Watching them on stage I had time to reminisce. It was not so very long ago, in college, that I was doing my second play with the Ruchika theatre group in Delhi. *Bhutto*, the controversial play written by I.S. Johar, in which I played the young Benazir Bhutto, got banned the very first day. We were in the wings, waiting for the curtain to open, when the news came in. But today backstage is where I had chosen to be—I had helped in the decoration of the Christmas tree.

The garden is edged by tall pine trees with the Ganga flowing on the side, and Swamiglee is penetrating me with a pointy gaze, like he wants to read something there. His eagerness to watch/have me perform is evident.

Why? Will I get paid for appearing on stage? Like we did on Bollywood stage shows abroad? A 'spiritual' payment, perhaps? Hmmm, what would that be. That's funny, I laugh at my own joke. I resist the temptation to say it, for I assume the patron might miss the humour. The brightest of journalists did, and the misquotations were not funny after a point. I was still reeling under the traumatic aftereffects of those insinuations.

His gestures and advances were almost like those of a little boy tugging at the skirt of his mother; he trailed me everywhere. And this just when, away from a shooting schedule, I was enjoying the solace of being away from unwanted male attention.

Is Swamiglee just pure curious? To know why I, a glam queen, left glam biz? Or is he attracted to me? He

Fire Island, New York,
1988 -- One of my first
International fashion
shoots. The photographer
was Frank Schramm,
a leading fashion
photographer in
New York then.

A happy social worker who believed we need to 'make love, not war', turned out to be a media and fashion darling of the late 1980s.

My closest lover, the
camera, has always
brought out a confessional
and curious honesty in
me -- as in these
photographs by
Ashok Salian.

SHANTANU SHEOREY

Above: Rubbing a bottle of Shweppes Indian Tonic on my cheek – all in the name of international fashion! The ad was carried in French magazine *Le Point* in 1990.

Top: A fashion shoot in Mumbai for Glitterati showcasing a Wendell Rodricks design -- the animal lover in me has fun with Pedro, the dog.

Showcasing Shahab Durazi (*above*) and James Ferreira (*below*) in an artistic shoot by Shantanu Sheorey.

Left: In Paris, a fashion shoot by a German photographer, with a French hairdresser, a Japanese make-up woman and a Lebanese stylist -- Wow!

Facing page:
Mirror mirror on the wall -- where is life taking me?

Right and below (left, centre and right): Three years after *Aashiqui*, I felt humbled by the fame.

Cover girl: My very first shoot in 1987, with gladioli in my arms, was put on the *Society* cover. Parmeshwar Godrej perhaps saw that and got me for a Marvel soap ad. Many covers followed from 1987 to 1994 before I made an exit from the glamour world.

Above and below: Chilling out not just after the fashion shoot but during it, too – in Ashok Salian's studio.

Above: Frazer Island, Australia – I walk into the river thinking, I am not just this glorified glamdoll...Who am I? What is my calling? Renunciation followed.

Right: Sanyas, 2001 – In self-contemplation, I found the answer within.

Yoga days: AnuFunYoga alleviates depression and makes slum kids happy.

Far right: Privileged to be a part of the first World Yoga Day celebrated in India, 2014.

WORLD YOGA DAY

Yoga - Transforming selves

21st June 2014

Strike a pose -- A yoga talk in Austin, Texas, before other alternative yoga therapists and researchers from around the world, in June 2014.

rests in a male body—nobody here born on earth, no matter how realized, is God. Besides, Swamiglee did not wear a tag on his arm saying 'Check me out. I am a realized soul.'

'I have been on stage too much—in front, for all to view. Now, given a chance, I want to be a watcher. Be just an observer and not a participant.'

I walk off. I am faster than the flow of the unfussy Ganges by our side.

His young yogic legs, longer than mine, are faster. When just a step ahead of me, he does a nimble about-turn and stops abruptly right in front of me, blocking my path—I am impressed by the way the body of the superyogi turns—it is the fastest, the most relaxed turn I have ever seen anyone take.

Wow, yoga. Suddenly, I am inspired. It is a far cry from the disillusionment I felt in the world of glamour—nothing was happening there that would have me jump off the bed each morning to go and shoot.

He is close, very close. But the red buttons of his black woollen jacket do not touch the pink peaches woven into my white pashmina shawl. Remarkable discernment—he has come close, stopped me in my tracks, but still respects the distance between us. I like that. Awareness.

He fixes his eyes on me, the dot in the flame of a candle. An intensity we learnt recently in the Tantric practice *Trataka*, inward gazing. A pause in his breath, the arrow question, is darted at me:

—Who are you?

The absurd question sets off alarm bells in me.

'Not who people think I am.'

I am an old tree standing on a hill top whose leaves respond to the wind and flutter, but my core stays grounded, rooted; it delights in the brush of the wind but does not get swayed by it.

A little over three months have gone by. He still misses the point that his sudden appearances halt my walking tracks, that his strange advances are a bit nutty. To ignore the much-sought-after sanyasi has never been my intent, but a public persona blinded by the public eye values aloneness.

My turn to ask a question.

'Who are you?'

Perhaps an irreverent question, new to Guruji, and I prepare myself for the worst. Hopefully, he will not take it as disrespect; it was not meant to be.

'A human being.'

The passiveness in the male voice was surprisingly female. His gentle non-assertive tone got me. So simply put. I am impressed. His body totally relaxed, motionless, very far away from the macho man flexing his muscles to prove his manhood. I am strikingly aware I had reached a completely new zone...

Our conversation goes silent. We soak in each other's presence, caressed by the winds of a deep understanding. To understand the mysteries of the untouchable zone, is new. There was nothing more left to say, in words, in language, in speech.

Time, the timeless, was out of time.

Awakening. Had I finally found what I was looking for? In the simple discipline of yoga, with a master of his senses—I could show him something, I would learn something from him?

7

From Anu to Ana

It was the start of the year 1998, the chill of a January evening. I had just recovered from a ten-day-long bout of fever. Swamiglee had sent messages to the House of Shakti, the girls' quarters, and checked on my status daily. That was sweet, but I could not have told him or anybody else that in an ode to hasten the path towards a superyogi status, I had overdone it. I had gone and done 102 Surya Namaskars (I had got inspired by Bade Swamiglee, who was said to do that many each morning), on the terrace on a freezing, misty morning.

I had missed my berry tree, the 'baby' I looked after—had someone been watering it? At this point I was flaunting my berry tree to Samadhi, a young model from Spain who had recently taken sanyas. With my hand stroking the twisted but curved trunk, I was showing her how unusual it was.

'Anandapriya.'

And again the familiar male voice from behind. Sounds like a spiritual name. Calling me?

'Hope you don't mind I called you by a strange name. Your new name, one that you were born with.'

Born with? Startled, I wanted to tell him off. But then, that is what a spiritual name is, I had heard from an Australian sanyasi; it represents your most basic characteristics.

I heard myself mutter, it was an automatic response—

'A strange name for a strange girl like me.'

Perhaps I felt it was too preposterous to want to change a name I had chosen when I was just four years of age. Apparently, at the time of my school admission, when asked for my name, before Ma could say, 'Anuja' (little sister to brother Anurag, Ma had thought), they heard a little voice saying—'Anu'. Ma and the alarmed school principal opposed it in their elderly way. But I would have none of it and had to be called Anu.

Samadhi was wonderstruck, and expressed wide-eyed disbelief. 'Wow! Guruji gave you a name? Without you having asked for it? That does not normally happen.'

I would discover later that 'bow down at your guru's feet and beg for deliverance' was the formula for success in the spiritual realm. But I had not declared he was my guru so it struck me as odd he had given me a spiritual name. I had not known then that spiritual names were given to people only when they asked for them, and it had never occurred to me to ask for one. What's in a name after all, as Shakespeare would say.

My spiritual name:

Anandapriya = the lover of bliss. One who loves bliss. Or is its lover. Or both.

From Anu to Ana—I did not know then how deeply I would start to associate with this name. That is the name/one I would remember in the darkest times of my life later, when I'd even forget my original name—in Life 2.

Three transformational months had passed. The quality time I spent at the yogashram had been wholesome and rich. Yoga had made me discover the richness inside my body. I was the closest to living in heaven, the happiest I had ever been.

And 11 January 1998, my birthday, would turn up the biggest surprise.

'Anu, you have a visitor.'

The building in-charge of The House of Shakti (we named her Swamibitteryogi, you will see why) looked like she was having a bad sanyasi day. There came from her an ugly breath of the kind jealous women had each time I walked into a party in Mumbai. I wanted to tell her that I was taught by the Buddha to 'Let go' but when I smiled, her eyes transmuted the feeling, 'Go away, you bitch.' So people who renounce the world, have those kind of feelings too.

Just yesterday, I had heard Julia, the yoga student from Spain, being told off by Swamibitteryogi—

'Can you stutter a little less, those sandals of yours make enough noise to bring The House of Shakti down. Remember you are training to be a yogi: totally centred and silent. Walk in peace.'

Julia was a model in Bogota. Bade Swamiglee, in his ode to integrate householders into living a life of yogic awareness, had ordained the parents of Julia into sanyas in 1971.

I had tiptoed down the staircase, wondering who the visitor could be.

Under the fragrance of a succulent rhododendron tree, with showy white flowers, stood the tall and robust figure of a sanyasi, Swami Yogarishi. Apart from the fact that he came closest to being a tawny supermodel, our Yogasana/Pranayama teacher always had a smile on his face—like a private joke was running through his head.

'Swamiji has called for you.'

Another summons from him, who hardly ever called anyone? It struck me that he was calling me more and more often, every day almost. And that in turn was generating a curious jealousy in the other sanyasis, especially the females, who sought his attention but somehow never seemed to get it—for instance, the Polish, tall-bodied Swamibitteryogi.

Under a promising sky with many hidden rainbows Swami Yogarishi and I walked. I was beginning to fall in love with the lifestyle yoga demanded. Exotic gerberas, the ornamental flowers from the sunflower family in yellow and pink, were aligned next to red roses; they lined our walk towards the patron's *kutir*. It was the first time I was walking with one of our teachers, in an environment where not much interaction was welcomed between students and teachers, especially between genders.

That Swamiglee had sent him, a male swami, and that too of the supermodel kind, to fetch me was out-of-the-yogi-box.

—It is World Laughter Day today.

Swami Yogarishi took a deep breath, let it travel down to his lower abdomen, and released it with full force—a hearty bellow resonating in the valley. It was a cold winter, so we wore our shawls, caps, ear-caps, jackets, sweaters, scarves, and inners. The laugh had the purity of mountain living and breathing.

I guffawed, too.

And our laughter softened as we entered the *kutir*, where in an orange and fiery mist of flames Swamiglee sat on the floor, the blazing fire from the *havan kund* reflected on his bare face, and bare chest. I did not know then that it was the most special day for Swamiglee, too—it was his 'birthday', the day he was ordained in sanyas and got a new birth was also the day I was born on this planet.

That he and I had a deep connection was undeniable.

Swami Yogarishi disappeared quietly, no formal greetings of 'bye' or 'see you' were exchanged. I was learning the way to preserve energy. I was starting to look at the city-ruckus in a new light.

Swamiglee chanted some Sanskrit mantras, while the spacious living room was radiant with a glow. Regally seated on a goat-skin rug he was delicately throwing some rare herbs from the forest into the fire. The dog outside the room sniffed, fell asleep, intoxicated by the smell of purity.

Later, Swamiglee led me to his bedroom. It was next to the four-poster single bed that he gifted (all offerings coming from Swamiji are called *prasad*) me a Schaeffer pen (how did he know it was my favourite?). There was no vocal exchange. The entire interaction oozed auspiciousness; it had an undercurrent of devotional sensuality. I had assumed the form of a goddess he adored. Next he pulled out a beautifully handcrafted emerald-green shawl and draped it on my shoulders; he seemed to be making an offering. It was done with the surrender that in Tantra a man must make to his Tantric partner, the devi. His still hands almost touched the back of my bent and bare neck. In his shaved scalp, a short black *lungi*, slim arms and a rounded bobble of a tawny face, was the superyogi still my kind of man?

It was a special moment. His mesmerizing stare conveyed the familiarity that came out of sharing more than our dates of birth. Our eyes had got locked and stayed that way, without blinking. His medium-brown eyes seemed to capture the quiet serenity of the *kutir*. I flew into a magical space while the fire in the *havan* behind us softened till all that was left was ashes, a paste of which he would smear on my forehead in a fine, horizontal line before I left his *kutir*. A calm descended on me the like of which I had not known before. It surpassed the erotic.

And then we were called to Samadhi Hall at an unusual time. Normally we reached there each evening at six, for the last assembly of the day, either for a talk on the Upanishads or the Gita, or a *keertan* session, or both. With musical instruments—the pakhawaj, sitar, dumroo, tabla, harmonium—behind him, he sat on the elevated platform. His throne was bedecked with fresh lilies and the candles running along the entire length were all the same size.

Swamiglee had a frosted eggless cake for me on my first yogi birthday. Was it to demarcate that I had departed from the callowness of natural human condition? Opened myself to the mysteries of the universe?

He called out my name. It was a pleasant shock.

Without a jerk or stiffness I got up, and remembered how just this morning I could touch my nose to my knees while performing an *asana*. The model's body had become incredibly flexible and light. I moved towards him. There was pin-drop silence. Seated on the marble floor, 1,200 sanyasis, yogis, and yogis-to-be raised their heads. I had become the focus of their attention as I strode towards the stage where Swamiglee sat. Even from a distance his eyes were penetrating me.

Swamiflusteryogi, the manager, could feel the bile in her stomach rise to her throat in discontent, her self-esteem shrinking. The manager could not help but start to harbour a plot to have Anu disappear.

The patron's birthday was one of festivity—there was sumptuous food, students and sanyasis did *keertan*, performed skits. But in all the fanfare I did not anticipate how this day of unexpected celebrations would mark my day of departure from the yogashram.

The best birthday of my life would end up being the last, in this life.

Six months had passed, and in the March of '98 the berry tree was abundant with ripe berries. In fact, it was bursting with lavishness; the entire cobble-stoned pathway had little berries strewn on the ground, as if the fruit had been ejaculated from the tree.

The idea of looking after a tree was to reconnect with our roots; we are closer to nature than anything else.

Just yesterday Swamiglee told me about the tree of life that grows in each being, and how we should be aware of the way the stem, the branches, the leaves, the flowers emerge; and the shape and the fragrance they assume. The Tree of Life that we, like little infants, were groping our way through. How interesting, I was tickled.

My time of adorning, loving and appreciating the berry tree was between 4.45 and 5 in the evening.

Swamiglee set the schedules. He set the timings. He decided where each person worked. I considered it fortunate that I was the only student given a personal tree to look after, as this was not a part of the course. Only swamis had been given their own trees: Swami Tripura got the pine tree behind mine, while Swamibitteryogi got the lemon tree on the other side, and each time I walked past her she had the disgusted look of a sour lemon. I smiled and that never seemed to agree with her, and in fact my happy demeanour would aggravate her sickly condition.

One day I had caught her hiding in the bushes and watching as Swamiglee passed my tree. And when he stopped and gave me a lingering look, Swamibitteryogi had not looked too pleased.

The next evening he again walked past my berry tree and was about to step into his *kutir* garden, where it was time for him to blow the conch, when I offered him a fully ripe berry to eat.

'I don't like berries,' was his crude reply. How un-yogic, Swamiglee. A superyogi is beyond likes and dislikes.

'You think you don't like it, that's why you don't,' was my quick retort before I turned and walked off.

Six months of yoga study, and I was ready to spread the word, and prescribe the dosage to superswamis and such.

When our course ended I was put in the transcription department, where I heard the tapes of the *satsang* of

Bade Swamiglee from around the world. The knowledge was precious and its scope immeasurable, so I took some personal notes too. Yoga had transformed me.

In Uttarakhand I had blown kisses in the soft, unpolluted purple-pink sky, I had thanked my family, friends, and all my fans.

When our yoga exam results were announced, Swamiglee called me on stage. When giving out the certificates, he added a chocolate slab as a gift to all A+ grade students who scored over 60 per cent—and lo and behold! I was one of the select ten.

And he leaned forward from where he was seated on a mat on stage; held his breath back, and whispered in my ear: 'Well done. Congratulations.'

'You should take sanyas.'

Swamiglee flaunted the fact that the ashram of his guru was one of the first to give sanyas to women. Badeguru had considered them capable, in the 1960s, at a time when most other spiritual schools barred women from becoming seekers of higher knowledge, from renunciation.

Bade Swamiglee had a light humorous touch when he pointed out, in a *satsang* talk I had heard:

'Women are our mothers. And you only know who your father is because your mother confirmed he is; only the woman/mother knows who really the father is.'

And in his *satsang*, the front two rows were always reserved for women, they were shown respect.

Swamiglee could see the renunciation in the yogi-nature of the movie actor. Even in the simple no-fuss yoga clothing she breathed of style. Style yogi.

8

'The Men in My Life'

I was not surprised anymore when he sent for me. In the months gone by he found to his surprise he could not reach me each time he tried—I had located areas, I had found bushes to sit behind where nobody could locate me easily, and where I could communicate with the invisible forces of nature.

In his office were seated a couple of other men in red robes; he stole a furtive glance at me, and signalled me to a chair.

And again I sat right opposite the stillness of the river Ganga. However exciting that might be, it struck me that none of us students in the yoga class ever planned to take a holy dip in the river. In the city we had been filled with stories of the contamination of the Ganga by untreated sewage and tannery waste. But from a distance the river looked clean like a slate.

Sitting on the same chair I did the first time I met Swamiglee, I realized how comfortable I was being in the yogashram. It had the kind of unconquered simplicity the big city was unaware of. And it really was some good karma that he had held me back from an inglorious departure. I had indeed fallen in love with yoga.

The other two tall sanyasis, software engineers from England who helped Swamiglee in his computer work, had left. Since everyone talked in whispers, the lowest of tones, I could not hear them when they were there. Conserve energy, don't just consume it. Cut down the noise pollution—talk softly.

—'What do you know about Tantra?'

We had a paper on Tantra as a part of the syllabus for our course.

—Tantra is the oldest existing human philosophy, or science. With the definition 'Tanote Trayate iti Tantra aahe', Tantra is that which provides liberation from human bondage. Tantra weaves the individual soul with the cosmic entity/eternity.

He nodded. And I heard the murmur of the bees in the rhododendrons outside, and I saw how his random questioning did not leave me feeling stunted anymore like it had when I arrived here. He was exploring my inner space, he took the mantle of guruhood seriously, The questions were aimed at peeling me off—he was digging inside my wants, fears, fantasies, dogmas, phobias, taboos, fetishes. I was the lucky one getting direct, non-formal education from the renunciate. I knew he was learning something from me, too, though I could not be quite sure what it was.

Since I came here, Swamiglee had refused to let me out of his sight, and as opposed to those numerous suitors in the city who chased me for a personal advantage, Swamiglee did it to awaken me from the illusion of the Maya we humans are entrapped in, and how we thus miss out on gaining maximum advantage from life.

He sits yogi-still, like a statue, his gaze still penetrating. I read a question:

'The men in my life?'

He lets out an embarrassed laugh, throws his head back, and looks thrilled. I had guessed the question that he perhaps was hesitant about asking.

I could not let him down. He recognized Anandapriya as 'fearless', one who had a 'curious honesty that overwhelmed him'.

—I am done. Each relationship was disastrous. The men came from diverse nationalities—white to bronze to black, different religious sects conditioned them. But they all showed me love, in their own way.

I feel fortunate to not have left a leaf unturned, or a button unhooked, in my exploration of sexuality, sensuality, or just an honest human connect with members of the opposite sex.

But why does Swamiglee ask me?

Is he going to lead me from Sex to Love to Prayer to Transcendence as laid down in the Neo Tantra?

How many times did I hear the men say, on different occasions, 'I have never shared anything close to what we established in a week, with anybody else.'

But I caroused on a different wind—I had never really felt that 'close' to a man I dated. There always was lurking some superior energy, call it God or whatever, and I was 'close' to that. It was my retreat, a sanctuary within. But who is it then inside me, I wondered. God? My higher self?

Now, that's who I really, really would like to get close to. And everything, every action, each little breath passing through me, has got to be devoted to that. Well, mainly.

'Two years ago, around the time I left the glamour business, I had started to question the egocentric existence that almost all people in the world live by. Especially celebrities that I was one of.'

His faint smile showed an appreciation, though I was not very clear what that meant.

Time and again, history repeats itself. Another time, a different place, sees another love affair. Lovers change. Nothing else is new. A snapshot of the men in my life:

—An Anglo-Indian muscular jazz musician, Rick was a drummer who drummed the beat of my heart in unbelievable crescendo—in room-temperature aqua and delicious vegetarian food.

—An American, Danielle, I met in New York. The Giorgio Armani supermodel for a couple of years lived in Paris, had an unbelievable abs-body, and a penchant for cooking health food—he woke me every morning to the most sumptuous omelettes and green tea; trouble began when he introduced me to his grandmother who lived uptown—marriage on the cards meant it was time for me to sneak out the backdoor.

—Christopher Welling, the cool-headed financier in Wall Street—incredibly successful, and a follower of Sri Sri Ravi Shankar, nothing ever fazed him.

—An incredibly well-read and knowledgeable and intellectual of sorts, Australian Jewish landowner Harvey, who was twice my age, shorter and thinner than me, wore silver trinkets...the blond-haired man had a thing for Jaguars, convertible cars and a childlike enthusiasm for lovemaking.

—Laurent, a French restaurateur and art gallery owner, smelling of the most exotic French perfume...he and I had a long-distance relationship, through phone calls and bated breaths.

—An English architectural firm owner, Garry Brown in London, who introduced me to the Columbian army march, showed me the multiple, creative and pleasurable uses an empty champagne bottle can be put to.

—A venture capitalist and harmonica player, Pats from Texas, who had a mouth so soft and a tongue that moved on the most intimate parts of the body in directions I never fathomed it could.

—A German lingerie-maker, Patrick—a man always supportive, with a rattling candour, and supportive of me and my doings.

—The tall and young-bodied Iraqi, Ere, who I met in Los Angeles—he communicated with spirits, had the sweetest manner of speech, and read me the Jewish Bible.

—Roberto, one of the top guys at the Fiat car company in Italy—he played the guitar and broke into Italian love songs in restaurants where he wined/dined me; he sang songs of female supremacy and beauty on the road, or in the TGV train, as he strummed the guitar.

—The most moneyed guy I ever met—Abdi from Nigeria, who wore the thickest gold chain and the heaviest twenty-four-carat pendant—on bright fluorescent, well-tailored shirts and straight pants of the same colour; who preferred the most natural sexual act to be performed with both of us standing up straight.

And so on...

It was not their pockets that interested me. My willingness to date a man surges out of the hidden, I want to go under the skin, beneath the tissue, cells and the like—to the inner space.

I have an inkling, that a loving heart beats in him, this particular one. That would urge me on to consider the man. I stayed with the man till I was proved wrong; then I began questioning my own innocent delinquency. Albeit the deadline was never fixed, but sooner or later this occurred:

Butterflies in the stomach disappeared; freshness and excitement of a new horizon in the offing got a beating; I was growing at a faster pace, and skyrocketing in the glamorous starry sky while my man was still finding it tough to get the sole of his feet off the ground. In a desperate act of possession he'd foam: 'You are mine...just mine...only mine.'

A slurp and a drool and his tense face shaking nervously were accompaniments. And so were his sloppy insinuations that I was attracted to another man; or men, whatever suited his fancy. The ugly possessiveness, jealousy, and insecurity of almost each lover was like the poisonous sting of a scorpion at the end of its jointed tail curled up his loving back.

For me, then:

Sadness. Disappointment. Fatigue. I needed so to be trusted.

What went wrong?

When we met we could not do without each other. Now we cannot do with each other.

When we met, we got lost looking into each other's eyes. Now we do not see eye-to-eye.

Doubts. Confusion. Blaming one another. Unhappiness. Mistrust. Doubt.

Brought back by the probing lightness of Swamiglee's brown eyes, I concluded my reminiscence, 'I had a rough time. I had searched for Love. And faced disaster.'

He said he was charmed by my openness: it is rare—a pure heart.

Without knowing that 'Free your mind' is the postulate of Tantra, I was already following it.

'You have a startling sexual energy, Anandapriya, and what is even more special is you are open, you have a broad horizon, you can look at an overview of things.'

He let out a slight giggle, his eyes stayed with mine.

'I am not telling you anything new. But you would be glad to know—this sexual energy can be used as a drive for a broader and more penetrating experience of your spiritual growth and development. Liberation can follow.'

He was serious. As he bent down to tighten his beige sandal strap, the back of the crown of his head was now before my eyes. Having known him for so many months, I now felt slightly less incredulous about his body movements. He could easily get into the foetal position, I was sure. And he stood three inches taller than me. That was without my Jimmy Choo heels on, of course. But a couple of days ago, we had been shown an X-Ray of a foot in high heels—the postural deviation and the physical stress placed on the metatarsophalangeal joints was a sickening sight. Does that mean I, a yogi now, will never wear high heels that were a necessity in each fashion show? Oh well, I love flats, and I am out of the glambizz.

Curiously receptive to the spiritual-physical moves made by Swamiglee, I had never experienced anything like it: spiritual physicality connected to the spirit rather than the body.

In sacred moments, in the evening, as we sat on the swing in his haven, the million clusters of stars radiated, and the still trees took notice. Swamiglee would reveal the secrets of his life, and pour them tenderly in my receptive ear. Like his childhood that nobody knew of. His dreams as a teenager, and the process of how he became a sanyasi were things that he never talked about.

One evening he confessed about the first girlfriend he had, a Russian, when a sanyasi, and how their relationship ended when, after much thought, he decided to stay a sanyasi and not convert into a householder. This was all knowledge I presumed nobody else had.

I did the listening, and talked only when he asked me a question, so as to enhance our Tantric endeavour. Besides, I wanted to be in the moment, and considered it insane to talk about my life as a star, which I had walked away from.

9

Sex in the Forbidden Zone

—Are you not a *brahmachari?* I asked.

It was a question nagging me. Ever since we began the Tantric study, I wondered how a proclaimed *brahmachari*, or celibate, as I understood it, proposed to have a sexual union? Even if the act, thus performed, had the marked advantage of propelling one to an exalted mystic union?

He laughed.

'Brahm = higher knowledge. Or Bhram = illusion, deceit?'

In the two Sanskrit words, just the spelling changes and the meanings are exactly opposite.

'I am the first "Brahm", one whose teacher is Brahma the Creator in the trinity of Brahma, Vishnu and Mahesh. He is the giver of knowledge. That is what my sanyas is to me, and that is the meaning of *brahmachari*.

It is Brahma the Creator, who has supreme knowledge, + achari, the teacher, the giver of that knowledge.'

—So why celibate then? I continued the probe.

—Perhaps because sex, the most basic instinct in a man, is overpowering enough to divert a yogi from his loftier goal of unification with the Supreme...Tantra, the oldest existing philosophy/science, uses sex as the most major propellant to rocket one into a union with the Supreme One.

Tantra is esoteric, teaching of which is restricted to a few disciples. It appeared that for once, Swamiglee had met an adequate Tantric partner; who could see him as a human being and not just as a guru who 'will jumpstart them to a higher realm', a giver of superior powers only.

...When alone we were not teacher and disciple, we were lovers, both on an equal footing—he prostrated in front of the Shakti with his hands folded and head bent in surrender and eyes closed. Without aiming to, I, the woman, had assumed the female role of Shakti, the superior one.

Each day was a remarkable new event. By each evening we gradually progressed. Touching, holding, caressing, patting, embracing, cuddling, hugging, fondling, rubbing were a part of foreplay that lasted five delicate months. Freshness of the smell of purple lavender, a freedom to admit to each atom that is a particle and a wave, a burst of poppies in scintillating love, thoughtful and thought-free together.

I can't take credit for any of these encounters. They

were all designed by him, meticulously. We were growing in association, the intensity increased, gradually.

Transcendence of body-consciousness when in a sexual act; go beyond the idea to breed, was close to the idea of becoming one not with a person but with the infinite—Super Consciousness.

He was unassumingly clear about what he was doing. He had the gentlest, most un-lustful way, which was completely new to me. Passion of love came from the unbearable lightness in the lotus of the heart, and not from heaviness of the weight of lower *chakras* where sexual organs, the wetness, and hardness reside. Heart met Heart. It was not just a reckless dick-meets-pussy or a yoni meeting a lingam, which is very far away from the love of the heart, the centre.

He never lost his breath. A *brahmachari* is one who has mastered his senses, I would later learn. All through the performance of the sexual act, not new to me, his yogic body never tensed. This was new. His facial expression did not change from start to end—it resembled the emotionlessness of the well-dressed and bejewelled man in a picture I remembered from the *Kamasutra*, the study of which was a part of my preparation for the movie *Erotica*.

In the wilderness, amid green grass hissing like a snake, and the last throes of the setting sun, in serene silence and unmatched purity of Himalayan forest air, his Alsatian dog Shambhoo drawing circles on my leg with his tail and looking up at me with loving doggy eyes, my back to the flat and bare yogic front of Swamiglee, him whispering 'I love your smell' in my ear—I flew. Eyes closed, head thrown back, almost touching his shoulder, lips unfurling to heaven with my heart in my mouth, I stood tall and together and light. Surrender not to a person, or to the act, but to the mood of the hills.

Suddenly, hit by a bolt, I am shaken out of the reverie,

—I have to go. The House of Shakti gates will be closed. It is 7 p.m.

In a rush. Down to earth. Out of his haven.

He told me later, he really liked my conscientiousness. Knowing surely well he was the controller, organizer of the place, I did not rely on him to take control, expect him to handle the situation, especially since he was the one who started this 'affair'. He liked the fact that I didn't depend on him. I took responsibility for everything—for my life, for myself and for my own actions. He didn't know I had mastered that act long back, what with living alone in Mumbai.

His unwavering gaze, his childlike eagerness towards me, his appreciative demeanour, tentacles of delight emerged from him and gripped me, each time he saw me. People around could smell the scent, and since each disciple wants to be the closest to his guru, hideous jealousies started among the sanyasis.

At the start of the sexual union
Keep attentive on the fire in the beginning
And so continuing
Avoid the embers in the end.

—Vigyan Bhairav Tantra

I had read that while transcribing a *satsang* Bade Swamiglee gave in Australia in 1986. Only now was I being made to understand that the eventual ejaculation, where millions of sperms shoot out of the lingam and die instantly—results in energy burnout, and hence is avoided. And that men who propose to follow the Tantric Sex idiom, have to prepare relentlessly for establishing the control, where they can tell the sperms to revert their outward flow, and go back inside instead of shooting out. These are serious practices, and must be really hard, I thought.

But it was fascinating to learn about the idea that sexual intercourse can actually be as far from the idea of sense gratification as a square is from a circle.

—Coming for our 'date' tonight? he'd sincerely ask with a meek smile.

—What time? I have to run back before 7.

And this is how it continued.

Some days he would chant Sanskrit mantras as he placed a hazelnut in the open cavity of my mouth; or blow heat from a fireplace into my form as he focused on my eyes. On others, he sat in front of a golden *yantra* blob, a geometrical figure in straight lines that met against a yellow sky, accompanied by a Sanskrit incantation, and made me a silent participant.

In the stunning landscape of rare trees and plants, I was mesmerized. In the translucence of the pure north Indian sky, Swamiglee had the most relaxed, alert, conscious, and priest-like way. His superyogic mental makeup was minus any kind of intoxicants or selfish, devious, cunning, conniving, or malicious thoughts— he came from a higher dimension; and he planned big—to teach humans round the globe the secret of their birth here.

When Mahashivaratri came, I asked Swamiglee about its cosmic significance.

'It is the darkest night of the year. It is the night Shiva made love to his consort Parvati.'

My Dhrupad teacher, Udai Bhawalkar, a senior student of the famous Dagar brothers, had given me a CD, on the inner cover of which I read that Shiva was the first to craft the veena. Apparently, the naked, sleeping body of Pârvati was his inspiration, and that is why the veena is shaped like a pear, with the buttocks and breasts of a woman.

Swamiglee invited me:

—Come to the *kutir* this evening.

When Samadhi heard I was going, she said, 'I was there last year on Mahashivaratri.'

Samadhi was not too pleased about my going. Then she kind of brushed off the topic with:

—Love your hair, can I comb it for you?

—Sure.

And off we landed in her room. On the top floor in Ganga View, the view from her room reminded me of the kind I had when standing on top of a mountain in the Himalayas—unadulterated space. Only now I was getting more in tune with the invisible beings that travel the sky. And how when we are filled with an internal benevolence, we attract that from the Universe.

We get what we give.

—So what do you do on Mahashivaratri in the abode of Swamiglee?

—Oh, you will see.

She refused to take her eyes off her hands that were caressing my hair, tied it into an egg-shaped bun.

Her disinterest in carrying the conversation forward was a bit alarming. A girl who normally loved chatting was falling quiet and avoiding a comment on this particular issue?

On the moonless night of Mahashivaratri, two flames become one.

That curious night marigolds decorated the path of the *kutir*. I walked feeling the closest to the superpower I had always looked for but never found. I was delighted.

It ended being the longest night of my life. We caroused in a moonless timeless zone where even time left us alone. It had seemed like a celestial party was in full swing. One I was attending after being invited for the very first time. Swamiglee was giving my spinal cord a rub—was transmuting lead into gold, transmitting his unbelievable reflexes, taking me on an astral travel.

It is hard to describe the magnificence of that night in words.

Lately she had been feeling feverish.

Yes, Anu is the cause of my heartsickness, huffed Swamiflusteryogi silently. She bent down to clear the walking tracks of a blade of grass and was instantly reminded of the efforts she put in to keep the place squeaky clean. It had not been easy to direct Indian workers who did not speak a word of Spanish. She had tried hard to learn Hindi to converse with them...Anu, on the other hand, was proficient in both Hindi and English, and had a way with the workers, who seemed to be in awe of her. Besides, she had fared well in the yoga course tests they had so far, so much so that the teacher of yogic history had held up Anu's answer sheet as a model for the other students to emulate.

Swamiglee's growing fondness for Anu was apparent. In Anu then, for the first time, the manager of the yogashram saw a threat to her managerial position.

Just yesterday it was the big Indian festival of light, Diwali. The swamis had been burning crackers in the lawn. All was beautiful. They celebrated Diwali together with Swamiglee. And he handed Swamiflusteryogi a burning firecracker in her hand, gifted her a new robe, they were both a bit flirtatious. And just then, her face ablaze with the bright light, Anu sauntered past. Lost in her own world. Where did she appear from? Swamiglee's attention of course drifted away towards Anu's swinging stride. He could not resist but exclaim,

—Van Kanya!

What is so special about her that in lieu of us sanyasis that stand next to him, he calls Anu the 'Daughter of the Forest'?

Swamiflusteryogi found herself entangled mercilessly in a web of jealousy, enmeshed in threads of low self-worth.

10

Thrown Out

It is an April morning. The sunflower seeds I had sown in the ground opposite the *kutir*, are sprouting raw buds of baby yellow sunflowers. They look as energetic and youthful as I do, what with eight months of scrupulous yoga training, and living a relaxed, stress-free balanced yogic life.

But that night was a disaster. Swamiglee was out of town. He had gone for a meeting for his dream project—a yoga programme for children under sixteen years of age. This was the night Swamiflusteryogi had been waiting for. There was nobody to protect Anu, and all the hatred she felt for her simmered in her heart like hot coal.

Number two in the yogashram's hierarchy, she ordered two sanyasis to throw Anu out, with a licence to use extreme violence, if needed, to achieve their goal.

They knocked on my door at night. Since no men were allowed in Shakti House of Women, I was taken aback when I opened the door—the next moment I was lifted and placed in a train going to Delhi.

I had no qualms about leaving—it was Swamiglee who wanted me to stay—but it left me shocked, shaken, and belittled. Such an act, committed by teachers who taught in a university of yoga, was so off the mark. It was like an assault, but the manner in which it was carried out made me feel like it had a racist undertone. In the name of renunciation what kind of devious thoughts do people, with heads shaved and holding no possessions, harbour?

And Swamiflusteryogi had stood in the background and given me a withering look when the car I had been dumped in headed out of the metal gate of the yogashram. I had been deluged with the sheer intensity of this violent hatred, but I found I had compassion in my heart. I wished them well. I found that my heart went out to Swamiflusteryogi as even in yoga and sanyas, she had not found a remedy, she had not found love.

However battered, I left having received the biggest gift of yoga—transformation. I was healed. Ready for the next level.

In Delhi, the age-old sehmal silk cotton tree outside the house looked robust; its red flowers had ring-necked parakeet feasting on the curved petals. Just the previous morning I had admired the same tree in the yogashram, which had shed its leaves and was laden only with flowers.

Pleased to see me, Ma, the only supporter of my unfathomable decisions and doings, asked what delicacies she could cook for me. Stroking my forehead with her blue cotton sari like she was clearing all the hardships of the yogashram, she enquired what it was I was proposing to do once I got back to Mumbai. This is what had bonded me to her—before suggesting what she thought I should do, she made sure she asked what it was that I wanted to do.

'Of course, teach yoga/tantra and a natural way to be. I am farther away from the world of glamour, Ma...in the last couple of months I have been thinking not of what I would like to teach, but what the city-dwellers really need to learn. It strikes me that out of all the practices I have learnt, it is Yoga Nidra, the psychic purification network, that would benefit people tremendously.

But when Ma heard of the sinister motives that led me to leave the yogashram, she was horrified. 'They will kill you! You are not going back to the yogashram, Gunnu,' she said, knowing little that in months to come, something would 'kill' me anyway.

Mumbai. Against the backdrop of the sea in my Worli flat, I woke up one morning asking what it was that I was really attached to, and could not do without. 'You should take sanyas,' Swamiglee had hinted.

I stood in front of the long mirror I had placed next to the door:

Was I really attached to family?

No.

Boyfriend?

No.

Idea of marriage?

No.

A particular rich, elitist life?

No.

Any favourite cuisine, food, or chocolate?

No.

Prestige?

No.

Power?

No.

Money?

No.

The look?

No.

Hair?

Maybe.

Chop it!

You are not your hair. You are not just hair...

Large multipurpose scissors with an orange handle that I had picked up in New York were finally pulled out to be used. In front of the large standing-on-the-floor mirror in my living room, I stood contemplating.

Chop. Cut.

Ear-length hair is new.

11

The Night Before

That October night I took up the invite by Ram, my architect friend from Boston, to attend a party, a rare thing for me. Curiously, I was even ready to skip the yogi routine of *mouna*, the practice of complete silence, between 7 p.m. and 7 a.m., that I practised without fail. Swamiflusteryogi's bitter grudge against me had left a stinking feeling in my heart. I had found some respite in teaching friends the practice of Yoga Nidra—how to sleep yet lie awake. De-stress. My favourite mind-awakening practice promised deep relaxation to city-dwellers suffering from pollution. Advanced followers of Yoga Nidra could even hope for astral travel! However, it pained me that I had left without bidding farewell to Swamiglee. My gratitude to him could not be denied. Had it not been for him I would not be a yogi today. I owed my inner transformation to him.

The windows of my Worli flat rattled, what with the thunder outside. I was aware of the loving calm inside me as I rearranged the red roses in the vase that trembled from the gusty wind. Each petal that dropped was love. So was there love in the leaves of the two exuberant plants on either side of the altar, in the passage between the two bedrooms. I was mesmerized enough to ignore the havoc nature seemed to be creating outside. I existed in a beautiful inner world. Magical. The happiness I felt was unmatched.

Unconditional love.

After the strict training in the yogashram on punctuality, that night I was ready at 9 p.m. sharp. Ram was late. When I called his house his servant informed he had just stepped into a shower. How typical of Mumbai nightlife—and then they shift the blame on the traffic.

We were going to a dinner party at the US consul general's house in south Mumbai.

Then in Patrick's tastefully done-up house the waitress had made me a target—'one glass of wine, you could have a glass' and she ignored my 'not-in-the-mood' refrain. After the yogashram I had nearly forgotten even the smell of liquor. And I did not miss it. Finally, I spotted a potted plant on the other side and accepted a glass. Pa had said once, 'I don't drink but it is rude to keep refusing...just find a pot and gently lower the glass in it when nobody is looking.'

I did just that and smiled at the thought of super manipulator Pa who respected others' feelings first.

So did yoga and I knew it was in my genes.

And on the first day of the month of October, in Patrick' flat, I had gone to the bathroom to pee.

The last recollection I have is that of sitting on a pot in the large dark green English-style bathroom. The wooden brown lid under my thighs feels slippery and soft. I am looking at my bare folded knees striking each other. I see my orange Calvin Klein jeans hang down my ankles and crumple on the white porcelain floor. My large metal silvery buckle is the shape of a heart, its sharp point touches the ground. My thoughts have gone to Swamiglee and the berry tree he gave me to manage. I miss the yogashram.

Suddenly, a loud thud. My hands grasp the orange of the jeans crumpled on the floor with both my hands in a natural protective response. I fling my head up. My breath stops. Uh! What? Who?

The deep brown-varnished bathroom door I had closed when I came in is ajar. My pee stops mid-way. In the second I debate whether to get off the lid and button the jeans up. I pull down the black weaves of the waist length t-shirt to cover myself.

Three boys walk in. They head straight to the sink facing the door. They don't see me. One of them places a small, white packet on the light-green shiny marble that cups the sink. The others look focused on the packet in anticipation and expectance. They are totally caught up and preoccupied. They do not see me.

I heave a sigh of relief and stand to button up; tufts

of short hair fall on my face. I do not take my eyes off the visitors. I am guarded. I don't make a sound.

The visitors are oblivious of my presence. Maybe it is the long stretch of the floor between us. Maybe they did not expect anybody there. Maybe they don't care. That white packet grips them more than anything else. They don't as much as dart a glance in my direction. Thank God!

As I tiptoe out like a thief about to be caught, taking utmost care not to make a sound, I see one of the boys open the packet. He stretches the paper and there is a small amount of a white powder. Cocaine, I think. The boy who opens the packet pulls out a 100-dollar bill from his trouser pocket, rolls it, snorts the powder up his fair nose. Cocaine, I am sure.

Peevishly, I try to reach the doorknob. My eyes see the back of their heads—one black, one blond, and one light brown. As I slip out, two of the heads turn up to look. I gasp at their shocked expression. I quickly step out and shut the door behind me.

I look for Ram, who I came with—I want to go home. Tomorrow morning's early wake-up call for yoga summons me—an attractive intrusion. I need to get into bed and get some rest. Besides, the loud boisterousness in the room is something I have outgrown—I ran away from the celebrity claptrap three years ago.

I cannot locate Ram. I choose the most creative sport till I do. I start a vigorous dance to the stirring pop music. Some other people sitting on the sofas in the living room get up and join me. An enthusiast dims the lights. Automatically, the large space around us gets converted to a dance floor.

This was before eleven o'clock. What happened after that is a part of the unknown. A mystery. My own life is a mystery to me.

12

The Destruction

The early morning was filled with a heavy deluge of untimely rain. Chowpatty, one of the busiest thoroughfares in south Mumbai, was under police security. The birth anniversary of Mahatma Gandhi was on a Saturday this time. Ironically, on this day of non-violence, Anu Aggarwal faced acute violence.

Anusual.

Returning home from the US consul general's party, Anu was lacerated by metal. Cut by broken glass. Pulped inside the grunting car that was shaken by the stormy wind. Mercilessly reduced to a bloody mass of defeated bones; crushed and cracked, Anu would still breathe, however sparingly.

The policemen were astonished when they saw the white Mercedes take three 360-degree James Bond-kind of turns before flopping down next to the turbulent sea. It was only when they saw a female body slither out of the driver's seat that they rushed to pick up her body, which looked electrocuted. Her feet fell on the broken glass of the windscreen; blood oozed out of her soles.

And later, when the insurance guys checked the battered car, they began to look for loopholes to save money as the smashed condition of the car meant full insurance coverage.

The doctor adjusted the stethoscope on Anu's chest. He had recognized her immediately. In unexpected October rain, in thunder and lightning, she had been hurried into the hospital in the wee hours of the morning. Four strapping policemen had held a luscious female body that looked opiated, dripping wet with rainwater, oozing red viscous blood. Under a sinking stupor and irresistible pain she was fading, but at the hospital gates she was still trying to stumble along, refusing to be lifted by the arms of the willing policemen.

It could well have passed off as a film shoot, but with no camera crew in sight it obviously was not. Was it drama in real life?

That day, the hospital had been bedecked with yellow roses—fans, friends, media, advertising and movie folks, were gathering outside Breach Candy Hospital.

In the Intensive Care Unit the hands of Dr Kartik were folded behind the white apron. Head bent, he examined Anu who lay there like a corpse. On a crisp white sheet she was wired down to the hospital bed.

Asleep in peace.

And even when Anu wakes up—if she does from the comatose state—her gestation period will be three years. Bedridden, the vegetable case will need to be taught the alphabet again. Death, in those three critical years, is almost inevitable.

Anu's clothes, doused in blood, lie crumpled in a plastic bag, like red-stained junk paper.

'You could throw them,' advises one of the doctors treating her at Breach Candy.

Pa is adamant as he says 'No'.

'I'll wash her clothes.'

With my own hands, he thinks bravely.

In the white hospital bathroom he stands crushed. An attentive glance at the crimson bundle reveals blood-spattered, orange jeans smelling of metal, glass, rainwater, rosebushes, and 212 Musk. Caught in the combined sentiment of love and sorrow, he places the strange colour of jeans cautiously under the open wetness of the ruthless tap, amid the scent of hard chemicals in the hospital sink.

Water gushes out and so do his pent-up emotions, in a spitting howl. Pa starts to scrub, with a fevered intensity, determined to remove the stain of the hideous nasty whack; the grossness of the event is worse than any Ma and he have ever experienced in their married life—he feels frozen.

Then, love overtakes like a fountain in spring and clouds all else—he is washing the blood, the excruciating pain his beloved daughter was exposed to...and is currently going through. Soothe her, he sobs.

A shock wave blows through his head; he tries to get a grip on what could have happened to Putri (his nickname for her). How did it happen? What happened in the car? She was supposed to have been behind the wheel. Or was she? She is injured—from head down to toe. Multiple fractures have paralysed her. Was she locked inside the car on the driver's seat...did she get trapped there?

He shudders at the inexplicability of the puzzling event. For once the agnostic Pa prays to God, the saviour.

It seemed just like yesterday that Putri was born. Eleven days, since the start of that year, had seen no sunlight. On 11 January he had been thrilled to get the good news:

—A daughter is born to us. Celebration!

Delighted, he shot off telegrams merrily, to family and friends.

The telegram seemed a bit odd to most of the relatives as only the eagerly awaited birth of a son, who'd carry the family lineage ahead, was officially commemorated in India then.

❧

Flat 503, Anu's house, wears a bare and sullen air without her. In the living room, light comes from a white crocheted lampshade with shining beads hung from the ceiling. On the polished mosaic floor two fading pink, silk lampshades, with batik embroidery in coffee-brown, stand opposite each other. Pa remembers Anu telling him about her trip to Aurobindo ashram in Pondicherry, and that is where she must have bought these. A ceiling-to-floor glass window is one of the walls in the hall. A frothy sea is visible from the window, just as striking as his beautiful poochikoo.

In the hospital—

Flat-pressed on the bed strapped in wires, titanium knots, I am inside the Intensive Care Unit. In a comatose state I lie 'asleep' in a space where fatality is normal.

Though unconscious to the world, I was alive.

Inside my head the slate of life lived so far, was being wiped out. An inner orderliness, a melody existed amid that external, physical chaos: transmitted to another zone, I saw angular harps played by horrific, twisted black creatures in an ugly splash of filth and stink in dungeons of darkness. Weightless fairies gleamed in contentment as they flew wingless in higher space.

The two stark opposites of love and hate exist in harmony. It is due to the light that darkness exists. And the meaning of balance was the acceptance of both the opposites.

This was not visible to anybody.

A calculated amnesia followed.

I could feel the loving hands of people, I could sense true concern, I appeared asleep to them but I lay awake inside my head, the inner optic lit. Coming from the innermost recesses of the being, the paranormal power of clairvoyance was awakened. I heard the subtle breaths of people, saw the chaos or the smiles inside the walls of the room, I knew more than what senses reveal. Bizarre.

Seemingly unaware of the smattered body condition, I was far away from the exteme trauma I had been through, just yesterday.

A CT scan detected many multiple fractures in the body:

Clavicle—multiple fracture of the right collarbone;

Humerus bone in the upper right arm—multiple fracture;

Unstable pelvic fracture;

Bladder rupture;

Jaw—multiple fracture, dislocated;

Basilar skull fracture;

Temporal bone fracture of the ear;

Ribs, mandible—hairline fracture;

Sinuses smashed;

Forehead fracture suspected;

In the orbital region that holds the eye, fracture suspected;

Nasal bone fracture suspected;

Inner ear fracture, causing labyrinthitis, a disorder of the inner ear.

Head injury: damage caused to the underlying blood vessels;

Brain bleed.

With damages so disastrous I lay painlessly asleep in the hospital's fresh linen. It was suspected I would cop it any second, it was a question of when.

On the last day of coma a sharp image was visible on my brain screen. Appointed my Don Juan, the libertine devoid of silly moral constraints, was Bade Swamiglee. He was a constant presence. The figure of Swamiglee in a dull red robe, standing some distance away in the background, was way smaller. Two sets of eyes sparkled bright as diamond dots in an earthly backdrop—focused intently on me.

—You, a yogi, can choose your own destiny. Yogis do.

A water spout, a slender twister, spins under the storm-streaked sky. A sound inside my head: this is a new birth, you are being cleansed, you can bring heaven to earth—within you and all around you.

Creation: A new Anu is to be born. Anew. A resurrection. Metamorphosis.

Ironically, it was a time when I was in the most sensually elevated realm.

I existed like in a celestial spacecraft with stars. I was orbited by the sun, the stars, and planets and beyond.

I had the joy of weightlessness.

I was, mercifully and mercilessly, thrown to merge with infinity. The Universe.

It was humbling, beyond words. It showed me the

most intimate link I have with all beings. Born of love, we are all love. We are all One. Love is all there is.

The first surgery was done to realign disjointed pieces in the cracked humerus bone, in the right arm. I do not remember the operation. What I do recall is the out-of-body experience I had during it:

Standing outside the lifeless body,

I watch an unrecognizable face,

A defragmented form—I am not in that frame.

The operation is being performed and I have jumped into a cocoon of darkness. The tunnel I am in is silky and warm. So dark I don't see anything. I am rapidly being sucked into the eddy. There is an absence of thought, I don't even ask where we speed to. There are no questions. I am moving very, very, fast. A sudden burst of beautiful light numbs all else. I have a perfect sense of belonging. I am about to merge with the light. I see the multi-dimensionality of the entire universe. My consciousness expands so far that I am not even aware of myself...In the instance I experience what I can describe as pure bliss. I have a sudden feeling of peace—vivid senses enrapture me.

I seem to have reached a 'point of no return' and do not want to return...

A 12-inch-long silver metal plate is implanted in me to support the broken humerus. There are eight steel screws around the incision, to hold it. Then the skin is needled, sutured and stitched up—twenty-eight horizontal stitches are visible—from shoulder down to elbow.

Apparently, in the next quick surgery, they gashed the skin, prodded all internal organs to check for internal damage, stitched up a ruptured bladder. A vertical mark resulted that looked like a serpent—with its head just below the breast, it stretched all the way down and ended with its tail just above the vagina.

'Lucky you. Your daughter has no internal breakages...the spinal cord is intact,' Dr Shekhar informed my father, polishing his glasses.

Pa heaved a sigh of relief: she will not be a Christopher Reeve-kind of a case—the actor who played Superman and who, as a result of a fall in an equestrian competition, had to have the base of his skull reattached to the spinal column with wire, titanium, and bone grafted from his hip.

'Only her bladder ruptured, but we surgically enclosed it. Don't worry, your daughter can bear a child, have babies,' Dr Shekhar assures.

In the current situation that is the least of Ma's concerns.

She wants to see her bubbly daughter alive again.

I wake up.

Dr Kartik exclaims in glee:

—You are alive! This is a miracle.

—Alive?

Was I not alive when, during the first surgery, I scanned my own body from the outside?

9 a.m. Light changes, that's all. They call it 'morning'. You exist regardless. You are a part of eternity. My eyes flash open to intense activity—three attendants in white uniform hurriedly wheel a stretcher into the room. Methodically, they adjust the stretcher parallel to the bed. There is an absence of sound. Everything is distant, far away. 'My' body, which I have no association with, is lifted. I curiously watch it being raised above the bed, and then placed on the sharp green of the stretcher. The stretcher moves fast down the corridor, then is stationary inside the lift.

I am motionless.

Delicate, like a newborn.

Filled with childlike wonder.

The earth a mystery.

We are in the Magnetic Resonance Imaging (MRI) room. The MRI is a type of scan that uses strong magnetic fields and radio waves to produce detailed images of the inside of the body.

The radiologist, Dr Anirudha, points to the image and continues:

A Computerized Tomography, of the base of skull, is performed; there is fluid in both mastoid air cells, right mastoid fracture is noted, right sphenoidal polyp is noted.

The conclusion: there is fluid in both mastoid air cells, there is a right mastoid undisplaced fracture.

Whatever.

The radiologist is exuberant. Kind in his clean white robe, his hand is uncomfortably hidden in the pocket. Nervous tic? What is he nervous about?

—Your body was knifed and shovelled, interfered with too much, and this broke the chain of any more intrusion from our side. The body at any given time can only take that much...your body took an unbelievable amount of poking, jibing, slashing, and slithering.

A pale smile accompanies his voice:

—Apart from the skull, there was a crack on your forehead, in the orbital region that houses the eye. We needed to recheck it for a fracture but we could not do it as too many other parts of your body required immediate attention...

That is why that area is shrunken, like a hollow cave, benumbed. Half the forehead is paralysed and is smeared with black ash.

And I cannot understand what they say—I have difficulty hearing.

The Bell's Palsy-ridden face does not show the inward smile. I live out of the body more than I do in it.

You can kill the body. You cannot kill ME. I am part of eternity.

They lift the motionless body and place it back on the caterpillar-colour sheets on the Huntley's bed. I am back in the bright sunlit room. What does 'my body' mean?

The half-paralysed body has advanced: from bedridden to wheelchair-driven. Facial trauma ensures the appearance of a completely relaxed botox-treated face, what with all the facial muscles paralysed.

The medical faculty discharges me. I am brought to 'my' house—I twiddle my thumbs at what 'my' means. 'My house?'

You go out for dinner one drizzly night but do not return; you disappear from your home instead. Return only a month and some odd days later and not know your house is 'yours'. And since you do not know you left it, you are not returning either. You are here as for the first time—you feel only a vague acquaintance with it. Amnesia skirts the film star, now worn-out, de-personalized. A special medically advised bed is what I lie on.

Dr Kartik visits, tells Ma:

She had hysterical post-traumatic amnesia. Damaged hippocampus in the brain means she will not be able to imagine a future, because when a normal human being imagines the future, they use their past experiences to construct a possible scenario.

Anu lives in the now, in the present moment.

13

An Old Suitor Calls

Faint rays of the November winter sun filter through the window, on which a tiny light-brown bird tweets enthusiastically.

—Rick is here, Ma says, bending down to clip her shiny hair in place.

Wired down to the bed I am immovable. With the inner ear damaged, I can barely hear her.

This morning she crunched an almond between her shiny well-polished teeth and I was totally amazed by the crunching action I am unfamiliar with. I am still on soups that are poured into a mouth that refuses to open because of the fractured jaw; immovable due to Bell's Palsy.

My body is in a state of 'permanent rest'. Harmonious surrender. I am glued to the bed but nobody knows I live mostly out of the body than in it. There are surrealistic dreams, accompanied by gods and demigods, in beautiful splendour of the heavenly.

There is intense dark I see, too. Dark and light exist together; they are friends. All is love.

And I am on Earth, a new mystery.

Who is Rick?

A tall, portly muscular man with the air of a youngster enters the room reluctantly. What does he struggle against? Nobody needs an invite to visit me. They come. They look sad to see me but actually most of them are despondent from their own lives.

—He is still in love with you, Ma would say. About a suitor she more than approved of.

She sounds like she is in a faraway land. The membranous labyrinth in the ear acts up, an inner melody goes on inside the ear, it dulls any sound outside. People wag tongues, only I have still to learn how to move the tongue, speak, shout, let it all out.

Standing at the door, not yet in the room but not outside either, Rick is saddened. A strange plastic smile decorates his face.

—Hey man, you will recover, fully. He tells me.

A fake enthusiasm shows he would like to believe it, but is not a 100 per cent sure. I understand. Nobody around is sure if I will pull through the disaster.

—Anu can do the unthinkable, he assures Ma.

He knows what I am like.

Having assumed a seat on the chair by the side of the bed, his gaze shifts to the gulmohar tree in the compound behind. It has just passed its flowering season. The tree leaves, in shades of sea green and tea green, minus the bloody red flowers, shine even without their mates.

At the first private screening of her debut film *Aashiqui*, he was the only one from her side who came, the only one a crucial part of her life then. And her family happened to adore him.

As an actor Anu showed her emotions openly. And that was exactly the opposite of how she was in real life. She was a hefty bag full of surprises. The media was wrong in a lot of their reportage of her, but they were right in one:

She is an enigma, he thinks.

He could never figure her out.

Letting out a faint laugh, he asks:

'So you were in the Mercedes Benz E class E230 with attention-seeking round lights...whose car were you driving?'

We have been out of touch for seven irrevocable years; he has not a clue as to what car I bought or the old one I sold.

A silver cap on his molar is revealed. A message plays in my head like a horn: there is a lot of unfinished business in this life for the being born in the body of Rick. Karma. Bondage. Some of the music inside the music maestro's head runs terribly out of tune.

From my heart, without speaking, as I cannot, I wish him well. I do not have any grievance against him. I do not even fully know him. But he and I are connected like all of us here are. Here on Earth. I am one with the Oneness.

'...How I wish she'd married me then, this would not have happened...I had asked her...'

Rick reminisces.

Yes, it was in this house. In that hall. Many moons ago. A receding waning moon shone dim in the window. Seated on the hazy green seat, on the *chattai* on the floor, he had proposed to her; for the last time. Then, as umpteen times before, in different locations of the globe, he regretted not having received a positive 'yes' from her.

And, of course, more emotional than methodical, he did not even consider the fact that he was barely earning enough even to sustain himself. It was beyond anybody's empathetic guess as to how he proposed to start a family.

A career as a jazz musician in India did not pay then; choosing it was a little like bathing in piping hot water in the middle of scorching Indian summer heat. He thinks of how difficult, how unfavourable being a jazz musician was, no matter how brilliant one was, and maybe that stood against her agreeing to marry him.

In 1991, jazz had such small fan following in India it seemed to be an unrecognized music category—the musicians found some recognition in making jingles for soaps, ceiling fans, paints, bikes and the like. And for this they got paid just enough for them to get by, without having to borrow money.

And that is what he had ended up doing.

Rick had succeeded in ticking love in that nineteen-year-old and he was flattered when she had approved of his love for her.

'Can't take you anywhere,' he had joked with her. Undeniably, Anu tended to create a ripple in any party he took her to. And this was way before she was recognized as a model or movie star.

But she did come to meet him at The Hague, for the North Sea Jazz Festival. The adventurous model insisted on a train ride from England. A wind of expectancy blew across the Amsterdam train station. He waited for her outside the station. That summer mid-morning had shone bright in the Dutch skyline. Some clouds of curious anxiety hovered. Anu's rapid success in the glamour world had been a worry. Did she still love him like she used to?

Love alters the entire human mindset. It creates a unique hunger for the love of the other.

All Rick wanted to do after she arrived was to head straight to his room in the hotel. Sure, he wanted to spend time with her. They had not met for a few months. Anu was always crazily unpredictable. After having earned in pounds, the latest fashionable designer stickers filled her bag. Her very first earnings, and the scents of Victoria's Secret hid in the lace of the sexy lingerie she had picked up. He feared her freedom.

Always one for fun, Rick remembers how she insisted they stay and listen to the jazz musicians play, on the road right outside the Amsterdam station. There was no denying the fact it made Rick slightly uncomfortable. Listening to the trumpet player strike a perfect note, he confessed silently, for the first time, that the fear of losing her nagged him constantly. Had she got it all too fast?

Then they went to the festival in The Hague. The most remarkable jazz in the North Sea was electric. It did not seem to matter if there was no vegan food available, they lived on salads and *batat frit* or potato chips, for that was all that was vegetarian in Holland. And Anu in her clothing derived from Indian tribal fashion drew all the attention. Rick rubbed his grizzly beard in memory of that time, his lips mute in a restrained smile.

In all that jazz, he had felt like a full-on rock star and even dressed a bit like that in his concerts. He had been true to his art. He sat behind his drums and with his wizardry would alter the temperature in the room—to a soulful one. The sound reverberated and filled the entire room, changing its vibe. He played the drums like his survival depended on it. An admirable passion for an art form was one of his first bonding points with Anu. They both valued the craftsmanship that went into any art form.

Anu was never one for half measures. She had started to distance herself from the outer world when she stopped signing new modelling and acting contracts. She has now perhaps taken that to the other extreme;

coming close to distancing herself from her own body. Here she is, flat-pressed on bed. Silent. Amnesic.

An unstoppable lass with a seamless footage of words, is wordless, finally.

He felt sorry that he did not wait a couple of years for marriage. She had proposed they wait for two years. But he was insecure. Who wouldn't be with a girl like her? In a deep breath Rick justified his act of marrying Kaya, a girl Anu did not know, without as much as telling Anu when still seeing her; he tried to soothe his guilt-ridden frayed nerves.

A leading German company had gifted him his first set of drums. For the then eighteen-year-old Rick, it was an undeniable and rare honour. The bright crimson drum kit, with its silver and gold cymbals, was magnificent. And he touched it, hit it, caressed it, and beat it. The drums were his tools to express the unflinching attraction he felt for Anu.

Enough playing practice had contributed to building those muscular thighs and strong oversized arms. Rick had not known that for her he was the manifestation of a dream man. And luckily, she did not have to kiss a thousand frogs. They seemed to be made for each other. Soulmates? The chemistry between the two was so palpable that each person around them was moved and got shaken by it a bit.

Rick, who believed in marriages being made in heaven, was clear she was his soulmate. And she was a great sport, open to adventures even of the sexual kind, her long Rajasthani *ghaghra* got in more than just the wind when they met. It was easy to go under the flowing long skirt, he recalls mischievously!

The creamy wetness of seductive, rip-roaring sex—they did it everywhere: in music vans, in local Bombay taxis in broad daylight, backstage, in stark badly-lit toilets of studios where he had band rehearsals, and of course, in his bedroom, which had an off-white rice-paper circular lantern (that he got especially for her when she moved in with him) dancing like a pendulum swung by the strong wind from the Bombay sea. They were too busy to ever think of putting the lights out...and Cupid shot arrows of full throttle of pleasure soon to turn into ultimate bliss—Ahh!

He opened a whole new world for her—kickass jazz licks, phrases, and patterns...

Miles Davis, Charlie Parker, Herbie Hancock, Pat Metheny, John Coltrane, Dexter Gordon, Becker Brothers...They put their heart in the music. And sang soulfully. He was not just an intellect-driven mind like the guys she grew up with—those in the corporate world who relied solely on facts and figures.

His first gift to her when they started to live together was *Sexus*, *Plexus* and *Nexus*, a trilogy by Henry Miller. She was quick to devour it, and shared his innate sensitivity. Other mornings Rick woke her up to Steely Dan singing 'Babylon sisters, shake it...' and 'Hey nineteen, now we can live together...'

Startled, Rick comes back to Anu and the single bed

she is lying on. Her eyes are fixed on the off-white ceiling, the expressive eyes not speaking, like she prefers the ceiling to him. Her eyes. Yes! That is what is so different about her. What a shame she is not present, she is not here.

14

Whose Reflection Do I See in the Mirror?

For months I stayed motionless in a room on the first floor, staring at the trunk of a mango tree visible from the bed. Then one morning I wake up. Have a shower at 5 a.m. In an automated response, I start the first basic yoga pose, pada anguli naman, to wriggle my toes in a paralysed leg. After a month of trying to persuade the toe, it finally flickers a bit. And this announces the start of my yogic healing.

A fresh, young, brusque doctor, tall and robust, sits squarely. With his keen eyes he has scrupulously followed my downward movement on the steps. As I reach him he gets up, still looking intently at me, scrutinizing my entire face. I did not know then that he surveyed the weak facial body tissue that produces movement.

His lips are sharp and etched out in a clear line. Dr Ashish sits me down on a dining chair facing the table. I close my eyes. I am light-hearted, I relax, ready for a miracle, with the innocent eagerness of a one-year-old.

'Let us reshuffle and wake up the paralysed face.'

And Ma and Pa are expectant—the dead plant will sprout leaves again.

The man with the puffy, pink face stands behind me, his thumbs touching the bottom of my ears. They start to move in a circular motion. His fingers are stretched out straight, palms open wide.

In yogic deliberation I start counting—1,2,3,4...We reach 30 and his hands move from behind the ears to the chin. His touch is close to the fractured jaw and I feel an excruciating throbbing, like an electric current. His invisible hand seems to be on a torture mission, it keeps moving slowly, touching new parts of my face. And then when he reaches the sides of my nose, I can't take the sting of the fine needles—I holler in pain, I bellow like a bull with a damaged shriek of a voice.

And I think—

Why don't you kill me instead?

That would be easier—to slip back into death—what with my acquaintance with death greater than that of the glory of staying 'alive'.

Twenty minutes later, the horrific session over, Dr Ashish goes to wash his hands.

And I remain glued to the chair, bewildered by this smarting experience, frozen like dry Christmas ice.

'Do this at least twice a day.'

Wiping his hands, his voice has the tonality of an adult talking to an errant kid.

Twice? No way!

After a short halt the doctor adds,

'Sit in front of the mirror...this is important.'

Why? was left as an unasked question. I don't know the language humans do. These killer 20 minutes had wrecked me.

Living in a deadened body, and traumatized, I get introduced to the feeling of incredible 'pain' in Life 2.

And the anguish continues day after day.

But I practise diligently each day with a question nudging me:

Who is this I see in the mirror? Is it a reflection?

Whose reflection do I see in the mirror?

15

Time for Sanyas

I did not understand numbers or how to punch them in on a phone but miraculously managed to make a call. My first phone call in Life 2.

'Anandapriya?!...'

He calls me that. He knows this name. He christened me Anandapriya.

Flags of joy unfurl.

I do not say anything. I cannot say, I cannot express what I feel. I don't know if I can speak any language humans do.

Silence pervades.

His excited emotionality besieges me. Electric currents shoot at a high voltage through the phone into my ear; one with the partial hearing loss. The other ear with serious hearing loss has a Bossa Nova kind of music, samba and jazz, beating inside the fractured eardrum. It is private in the sense that it is music that only I can hear. An instrumental piece that plays 24/7, does not end. Behind the partially punctured lungs, and a fractured ribcage, I hear the beat of my heart—it throbs.

Unconditional love oozes out of his astral heart. He purrs into the electronic instrument of communication, the phone. Both earbuds feel love pour in—the scarred one that bled profusely, and the other ear that felt the impact, and got partially damaged.

'How are you?'

He is keen to know. His relaxed voice soothing in its curiosity.

Even with the impairment in speech, a cracked jaw and palsied lips, I manage to blurt out pieces of the melodramatic tale.

'Why did you not call me? I'd have come!'

Would have been difficult to call when I was in coma, huh! But he is comforting. An anchor.

Before I can tell him all about the cellular explosion in my head and Bade Swamiglee urging me on to begin Life 2, he yells in excitement—

—Fabulous! Bade Swamiglee? This is a rare occurrence, happens to a chosen few.

—Hah! Am I the chosen one?

—How are you, Agapeto...Where are you?

In his voice, a soft serenity—his excitement inundates me.

I hear a whisper inside my head—Agapeto is 'beloved' in Spanish.

He was quick to pay a visit to Mumbai. A damaged physical condition but her spirit was more alive than ever. He knew then Anu had been to the Other Side, which superyogis do extensive *tapasya* to reach.

'When are you coming for sanyas?'

Since he does astral travel—will he fly and pick me? I laughed but my palsied face did not show it.

People loved the natural pout of my lips, my smile.

Even though I do not remember even my mother's name, I have a vague feeling the 'sanyas thing' has been long overdue.

Sanyas is the ultimate marriage between a guru and a disciple.

Oneness with infinity.

At the Bhattacharya household once again, on Carter Road, where I had had the first meal when I arrived in Mumbai: fried chips of salted green lady's fingers in mustard sauce. Delicious.

It was June of 2001. Aaditya had just returned to Mumbai from Italy, after having two kids with Victoriae. The Italian girl with an upturned nose and Aaditya were so busy making children they had not found the time to tie the everlasting thread of marriage.

'Where are you going?' he asks.

I was seeing him after many years. On being told I was taking sanyas, he commented,

'A course, created especially for you?'

There was an impish look about him, he was being funny, but I knew he was not joking.

He claimed that the course of the life of men changed once I entered their lives. That I was special and I could not help it.

Aaditya had been a witness to the drama between Rick and me.

He suspected the patron in the yoga place to have given in to my charisma. And that life for the 'poor sanyasi' would never be the same again.

—You have a background of caring for people. Remember when I first met you? You were training to better the lives of the poor, make a social impact. You worked for the empowerment of Muslim women in Jama Masjid. You counselled the mentally disturbed in the psychiatric ward of Lady Hardinge Hospital. You left home and lived out of a bag for years, in your teens, you were searching for the Truth then.

He added softly:

—You don't need to take sanyas.

But I prepare the irresolute whopping mind to go for the unpredictable—sanyas this time. I am ready to shave the regal hair in sanyasi ruthlessness, knowing little the battered skull had become soft like a baby's.

Prepare for, and surrender to service—let that be my ambition, if any.

16

What is Sanyas?

A year and eight months after the start of Life 2:

Do not forget, you are a sanyasi. You have shaved off your golden locks. You live out of a rugged bag. You have no home, no room, no personal bed even. You eat whatever is given to you. You do not buy anything from the market. You hardly leave the yoga campus. You do not keep any money. You have no possessions. You do not wear any jewellery. You wear no make-up. You have broken all ties with friends and family. You do not keep a cellphone. The landline is not available to make calls. If anybody calls you, you never hear of it. Solitude.

Residing in the spiritually isolated realm of the yogashram, with no outwardly luxury distractions, and all communication with the outside people/world singed, one has no choice.

What do you do?

With chattering strictly prohibited, you fall silent.

A lot of it was nonsensical—but hey, you are a sanyasi now. No complaints. Know thyself. Which, you pray, is more than what first meets the eye. The journey to know your Real Self begins.

Sanyas is complete abandonment to achieve complete totality.

Let Go.

We adopt Dashnami sanyas, where renunciation and non-attachment is promoted. Adi Shankaracharya, the forward thinker, the maverick, defined sanyas as a state of mind.

That's funky. Mind your mind, babe.

To put a previous life to flames, on the first day of sanyas, we performed the ritual of ridding oneself of hair on the scalp.

Burn those karmas stored in the hair. Start afresh.

Our heads were ceremoniously razor-shaved.

Even though my head did not bleed, it felt forced. A weeping trauma inside the head was revealed. It was like, without my consent, the tooth of the trauma wolf had cut into me.

I had been left plain helpless. Raped by rain, metal and glass.

Muniram, the old barber, entered the gates of River View, the official building of the yogashram, once every two weeks. In those couple of hours, unrelenting, he scraped innumerable heads off any visible hair. His workman's stained, white-cotton *dhoti* folded on his sticky thighs, Muniram sat on his haunches. His dexterous hands, raised and clipping away, built up a large bed of white, grey, brown, and black hair curls. A mass of filaments—Dutch, English, German, Indian, American, Korean, Spanish, Japanese, Swiss—piled up around his unmovable frame. We took turns. The Ganga a silent witness behind his back.

In Hindus a woman shaving her head is considered an extreme display of shedding off her womanhood. In the old days, women who committed sati at the funeral pyre of their husbands or grieved as widows, shaved their heads.

'Ego comes from an identification with your look, the form.'

Surrender.

Give your hair away to begin with.

We are then led to Samadhi Hall. Here, one can meditate to find the blank inside the head, the perfect union with the Supreme. The impeccable cleanliness of the pale-yellow floor was striking. We the newly born chanted a mantra and had Guruji bless us with a sanyasi's red robe and a slender burgundy shawl.

I found that most people who opted for sanyas were those rubbed the wrong way by life—like Kiki from New Zealand who had been bruised and beaten up in a nightmare of a marriage. She was done with the world. She was ready to pledge an everlasting, unflinching commitment to a better self, and to connect with the superforce that would never let her down.

Living a simple life is great. It actually takes away the unnecessary baggage.

But just one restroom, next to the dormitory all twelve girls shared, was tricky. At 3.30 a.m., the sanyasis stood in a queue to get ready for the first session that started at 4.30 a.m.—the Nada Yoga (the reverberation caused by sound). Long corridors, filled with a hushed silence, were reminiscent of Breach Candy Hospital. And twelve girls in a queue, waiting for one cloakroom, was a bit overpowering. I found a way out. I decided to wake up by 2.30 a.m. That was brilliant. The entire floor, in the pitch-black darkness, was mine. All mine. Not just the sanyasis, even the animals were asleep. Super!

And I was fine without hair, too.

'Maximize your potential,' was the call of yoga I took then. Sanyas was just stamping that card with an assurance.

Live in the Now.

Reverberate in your highest frequency. Dig deep to find the hidden treasure of peace in the innermost crevices inside you. Then share it with others. This is true love.

Love is all there is.

Under the watchful wings of Agapeto (Swamiglee), I watched the senior sanyasis very closely. And since I was their junior now, they felt free to inflict their sanyasi frustrations on me. Female jealousies got jacketed in a show of righteous sanyasi conduct.

With the seventh sense aroused—I could see that sex, or perhaps the lack of it, was the biggest chopper for most.

Like on one warm August afternoon I was looking up at the sky marvelling at a fast moving cloud, when a villager with his chequered *dhoti* folded up pulled my gaze. He was frogging up the entire length of an old palm tree. I looked at him gallop up—in sheer astonishment.

The tall PalmTreePose, who had come from Australia eight years ago and shaved her golden curly locks and vowed renunciation, was passing by, and took notice of Anandapriya. How un-sanyasi like, PalmTreePose muttered in disdain.

Her scarf-covered Machiavellian head was quick to spread word about the 'imaginary sexual thoughts' Anandapriya had when staring at a 'man'—the coconut tree man—and the need to set her straight.

She is sensuality personified. How can a sensual-sexual being be a sanyasi? Her openness permeates all boundaries. We always knew it, they hummed.

If you put your mind in what not-to-do, you will end up doing it more!

Grow up, sanyasi folk. One day, they will know how

baseless they were. And how crippling this attitude is in spiritual advancement.

I decided that with all their bickering over trivia, I'd still treat the sanyasis with love. And let this nourish my inner lotus. For lotus, though rooted in mud, never allows even a drop of water to change its beauty.

Knowing little about her speech impairment, he is taken aback by Anu's lack of response. It was not that many seasons back that her quick response always began with a smile. The smile came before the words did.

But now, as waited for her to walk past him and then asked—'How are you, Anandapriya?'—she looked him straight in the eye—not a grin even, did not even nod her beautiful bare head; just walked off from the palm tree shading him in the summer month of Uttarakhand.

That morning a fire ceremony to appease the environment had just got over. Chucking some rare forest herbs and ghee cream in the fire, he had been looking at Anandapriya, who sat in yogi lotus pose, her eyes closed, meditating. Then, the burning blaze of fire, the smoke, kind of dimmed her view of him sitting opposite him at a distance. He recalls the time when, in a similar setting, among more than a thousand-odd people, their eyes would be locked in an embrace. She was always there, waiting for him, with him. Her inner consciousness intact, she didn't just look ready for a leap into a higher dimension, she was *there*. No doubt now she has seen the Other Side, but she does not smile; she does not talk either.

That was unacceptable.

❦

One warm afternoon: In the outer corridor of River View, some sanyasis were bowing as they passed their guru. They were looking down, were quiet and walked with the least bodily movement.

Most sanyasis were given only one department they could perform Karmayoga in. Even though still adjusting to Life 2, with feet of clay, the belief of Guruji in my potential was evident. I was the only one to be entrusted with several departments.

So it was that day:

With numerous files that were hard to carry in a shaky hand, I ran past Guruji, without stopping to acknowledge him.

The sound of laughter behind me made me look back and I was stunned: With a contorted face he copied my 'model' walk.

I was chosen to catwalk as I had the right walk; it was not that I learnt to walk to become a model, or became a model and then learnt how to walk. Sanyasis around me stopped and enjoyed the entertainment.

He was tardy and cartoon-like funny. Hilarious.

He doesn't really know, does he? I laugh, too, but lo and behold! my face does not display the grin, stays static.

Where is Anu's humour that he loved so much? He wonders—this hit has broken her funny bone too?

I touch the black scarf. I pull it down over the forehead, tightening it. Hot tea at 6 a.m. in the biting cold is more than welcome. As I sit on the pavement and drink tea, I marvel at the beauty of the loosely-knitted scarf. Bhanu Athaiya, the designer I chose for my first movie, *Aashiqui*, got this black woollen scarf from Russia. It was her prized possession, but she had given it to me. Pulling it in my hand, I felt gratitude. It made me feel special that she had felt close enough to part with a thing so dear to her. For me, then, living in Bombay, away from family and home comforts, this love was much needed.

And this scarf had got added to the array of woollen, straw and crochet hats I had bought abroad. It had finally come handy. It was black, a colour, Sri LotusMountainPose had informed me, was acceptable here for a sanyasi to wear.

Learning to accept abuse, insult, and injury humbly is the thing in sanyas.

The frosty morning gave way to warm sunrays. As I scurried around, by eleven o' clock, the wool in the black scarf was heating up. Feeling uncomfortably hot, I remove it. Off it goes from my naked skull to the dhurrie on the dust-laden floor, where I sit.

As I eat lunch that day—

'What were you wearing this morning?'

I had just placed the first morsel of bread in my mouth. I had a vague inkling the question was directed towards me. Agapeto stood facing me with his eyes burning amber, legs aggressively apart, and his yogic, perfect body assuming an accusing, questioning posture.

I gulp down some water to drain down the dry morsel in my super-dry mouth; in my shocked state it falls out of my mouth. Some of the sanyasis around me curl their upper lips in disapproval.

What does he speak of?

He shouts his voice off.

'Why were you wearing that wig?'

His unexpected belligerence unnerves me, stealing any yogic relaxation I feel. Wig??...

'Yoga says we should not talk whilst eating.'

My speech is a wispy drawl...Wig?

Can we talk later? I want to plead, but cannot...

He does not pay heed to my unsaid musings.

He is cantankerous, and oh so unbecoming. Is it my casual, friendly tone, in front of other sanyasis, that annoyed him? When he addressed others, they normally either stood up to show respect, or looked like a giraffe had swallowed them.

'They say when you take sanyas you get married to the Guru. He can abuse you but it is all for your good.'

Gosh! Had I thought that divorce would become a spiritual liability? Ha ha. In showbiz, I had refused to wear a wig even when offered extraordinary sums of money.

His blame makes no sense.

The winter breeze makes me realize he refers to the scarf; it hits me with razor intensity. Funny that he, by mistake, I hope, considered a scarf a wig.

I need to tell him that it was not a wig but a scarf. And I cannot. I don't even stutter, and my lips are motionless from Bell's Palsy. My broken jaw gets locked with tight screws.

I cannot speak. Brain does not as much as send an impulse. I feel unfit to verbalize anything that is appropriate. I see a large blank in my mind. I see innumerable words fight outside the gateway of the mind. Each wants to get in first, but entry is denied to all.

I am dumbstruck. I am unfit to explain. Words like scarf, tassels, Russian, refuse to appear in my palsied head.

Caught off guard, I start to gag like someone is throttling me. The heart, silent in yogic regimen and solitude, is ripped by shock, and starts to throb in an unbelievable crescendo.

This is a misunderstanding. Or is it some weird impression he has about actors wearing wigs? Or is it his personal hatred for wigs that is showing up? Or maybe, he misses hair as he shaved his head—he became a sanyasi when he was just four years old.

He continued yelling, movies were thrown in, the

cheap and irresponsible nature (bullshit, I thought) inherent in all actors was highlighted, and he yelled and swore and he almost fell breathless shouting.

I am not a movie star today...

Two things became clear to me that day—

1) That even when a being is supposed to be, and is proclaimed, as enlightened—he is not God. There, I saw the follies of spiritual organizations and gurus. And then, I was not trying to get a New Life like normal sanyasis do, I'd already got one, hard-hit as I was by my New Life. I was already born anew. Life 2.

2) I am free to leave. I can leave right now. For Anu leaving was always easier than staying. She would have just got up and left. To return home or maybe not to this fretful stupidity in the name of sanyas.

I suddenly felt dangerously capable of doing that. I knew I could leave...right then if I wanted...I came dangerously close to doing that.

But a voice inside me said:

Let us do something different, let's stay—endure.

It seemed impossible that anyone could endure such harshness. This was a side of their guru the sanyasis sitting cross-legged on the floor got to see for the first time. Anu did not need to take this unexplained insult; the provocative star would certainly leave, they thought.

'Come.'

On the terrace, in his penthouse: a gateway to heaven.

The windows on three sides reveal forest lands, mountains—delightful views over undulating countryside.

A hypnotic sky.

'Out of thousands of people I have seen, you have a rare gift of sanyas.'

I know he means spiritual aspirants, his disciples, as well as yoga enthusiasts. The appreciation is a rare phenomenon. The Master, who draws from a higher source, is normally quick in pointing out faults in sanyasis.

It hits me as a thunderbolt—the 'wig thing' was a test. Like the final sanyas exams most sanyas postulants topple and fail in. That I stayed on showed my ego was a little smaller than the cosmic realities I had surfaced with. What a freaky test, Agapeto! Could have never thought it was one.

Thank you! is not verbal but thought waves are relayed between us. We are on the same frequency, the same radio station.

Like in mantra chanting: first you express gratitude by a verbal chant. The next stage is you mentally chant without verbalizing it. It becomes a wave in the third, and transmission is on a higher astral plane. In the final stage you become one with the source.

He invites me to live there permanently. He offers me the highest position.

He throws ideas at me. He gives me freedom to choose.

In the village, start my own yogi project for old

people. Start teaching young nubile girls the way-to-be. Aid in yogic education of tons and thousands of kids between ages five and fourteen...

He trusts me enough to give me freedom—to help people under the yoga wing.

Off my bent knees I lie with my back straight on the floor, legs stretched straight. Raising my robe to the ribcage I expose the 40-inch-long scar, carved on golden-brown, marshmallow skin. Like I used to open up with my mother as a child, I share with Agapeto my cuts, where I was knifed by scalpels and then stitched up.

His supple form wastes not a second and he leans next to me. With the concerned look of a cat with her baby kitten, his response is quick.

Love that animal alertness. It is of the kind that began my own search for my own alertness.

The yogic slim fingers stroke the serpentine mark on my belly...the caress is tender like he wants to heal it through touch.

I get up. I straighten my robe. I tell the golden swan about the girl from the advertising agency who followed me on the flight coming here, offering me a modelling assignment—to endorse Cartier watch.

'I'll model for anything that is yoga-related,' and shrug my shoulders.

He is pleasantly amused to hear me sound more like the Anu he knows. That is more like Anu. She is strong in what she does. He admires that about her.

A tight hug of reassurance is given and I am packed off.

The idea of devoting life to selfless service is an enchanting one, and like a rocket I blast off from my launching pad to complete the last pending chore—rid myself of my last attachment—sell my property.

17

Pulled Back to the City

On the mid-morning flight from Dehradun to Mumbai some passengers look at me curiously. My hair right now is way shorter than ear length.

What did I gain from sanyas, I ask myself.

Amid the pure endlessness of the Ganga and the scenic Degirivan, certain basics were made clear:

I have the mindset of a person who is not needy, not really. Therefore, one who is ready to give.

One who has little expectation to get anything from fellow beings, or life in general.

One who trusts she is looked after and hence no man is needed to look after her; if in the moment help is needed, the right man will appear.

My physical condition is not at its very best still but I have the strength to put my feet down (both my feet almost touch the floor now), and I have learnt how to converse, though not fully well. I am on the road to a miraculous/marvellous recovery.

Got the X-ray results. It looks brilliantly together. The broken humerus in the arm has realigned. A yogic union? I joke inwardly.

'Let's remove the scaffolding in your arm...you are too young to have an external piece of metal in your body; besides, it is not needed for support anymore,' says Dr Kekoo. 'The arm stands on its own leg,' he adds, laughing. He is obviously happy at the quick recovery.

Ideally, I'd have liked to have the mini-surgery the doctor was suggesting (nothing like what you've been through, girl!) without anaesthesia, but the doctor is horrified.

Anu can go beyond pain.

On the hospital bed again, the effect of anaesthesia wearing off, I wake up.

In the dark and dingy room the air around feels clotted. Unexpected heaviness.

But when my gaze meets my meddled-with arm, horror strikes. A mega-sized bandage runs from the shoulder down to the fingers!

Why? Even after I'd been operated the first time, when they inserted the rod, the covering plaster was only half the length of this; it was only from the shoulder to the elbow.

The heavy bundle covers the resistance to doctor's cuts, jibes, and slashes by scalpels on an old wound.

The fatty sheath around the nerve fibres must have resisted.

Darkness descends. I am home again, and the sea splashes waves of change.

Next evening: outside the doctor's home-clinic on Malabar Hill, creepers decorate a jaded brick wall. Sundried clay. I sit facing the doctor rather than lying down in a surgery room. The sturdy doctor is stiff, nervous.

'You know...when I split the skin of your upper arm to remove the metal silver implant, the connecting strings were in a zigzag, and not in the place they should have been...'

The child in me takes over. See this as a drama. Hah. He hides his quiver.

'A nerve got cut...I didn't know...couldn't see it...'

What?

You cut a nerve?

You are not serious, doctor...tell me you are joking. This can't be true—

A billion needles poke me.

Tell me this is a nightmarish dream.

So under an oversized plaster Dr Kekoo cleverly hid the nerve damage. Clever but not so clever.

He knew he had paralysed my right arm. In the surgery, he damaged one of the five principal nerves: the radial, a single nerve group.

This nerve provides a common pathway for electrochemical nerve impulses that are transmitted along each of the axon nerve fibres. Running from upper arm down, the nerve is responsible for wrist and finger movements. With a dysfunctional radial nerve, a 'wrist drop' automatically follows:

So, if I closed my eyes there was no thumb. I had no first finger. No second finger. No third finger. No fourth finger. No tiny smallest finger. And I had no nails. I did not have a palm. I did not feel the skin on top of my palm. I had no skin even above the palm. My wrist was decapitated. I had no hand and no lower arm. I had no elbow. I had no upper arm. Hopelessness was gripping my fragile mind. Again. Three years later.

I have been rammed again.

This too shall pass.

Go deeper.

I meditate.

Go deeper.

Reach the void. Reach the silence.

Next morning, a beautiful Dutch plate made of eggshells, with red roses and light green leaves etched on it, is going to Dr Kekoo.

A gift. To ease his grief. Nobody believes it. He doesn't show it. I know he feels it. '*Maan gaye tumko,*' says my mom. '*Jis aadmi ne tumahri haani kari hai, use tumne tohfah de dia? Bhai hum to nahi kar paate...Tum vaakayi mein sant ho gayi ho.*' (The man who caused you harm, you went and gave him a gift? This is admirable! I'd never have been able to do this. You truly have been transformed into a sage.)

I smile shyly. I did nothing. I am not the doer.

Expand the breath between the outgoing and the incoming breaths, just watch the distance between the outgoing and the incoming breath, simply watch.

One day, after a month's practice, my breath stopped completely. During a long pause between breaths I entered a deep, peaceful state, and felt I no longer needed to breathe anymore. Suddenly my entire body shook, and vibrated like the energy inside was being whisked by an eggbeater. I continued to watch it like I would from the outside.

Was this an extension of the out-of-body experience I had during my near-death-experience/surgery?

The silence so intense it penetrated the body. Suddenly there was an explosion, an orgasm, and I watched myself catapulted into the space around me.

In renunciation I had already been living on a strict regime: no eating of solids after 12 noon, a meal a day, no lying, no cheating, no sexual misconduct, no drugs, and pure discipline of silence in what you were given to eat and when.

Since this was a thousand times more orgasmic than the best sexual orgasm I ever had, being celibate was just fine.

And Karmayoga performed with that altruistic feeling was stupendous. Suddenly it mattered little if I could tell someone this or not.

In Mumbai, I am bombarded by the thought: am I still selling the property? Even if I do not return, for whatever reason, to the yogashram. There was not a single person who was in favour of my selling the flat. Why don't you rent it? Could be an option, but however foolhardy it might sound, the idea was to rid myself of the last attachment, to prove my sanyasi non-attachment. The sale of the flat is pending. I am not attached to the property, and still living, thinking as a renunciate. Karmayoga will continue wherever I am. In my last conversation (I had no inkling it would be the last) with Agapeto, he had said, 'You can live anywhere now...but come live here...'

The damage to the nerve and the arm is healing but not fast enough; you want everything faster than the speed of light! Hah. I refuse to be rattled by this life-changing chain of events, I skill myself with new helpful tactics:

I practise and learn to use the fork with my left hand.

And I find that pain brings an awakening too, and to awaken the self is the highest form of awareness, say the Sutras.

The next morning I walk to the building office. I

intend to inform them that Flat 503, Godavari is for sale.

The cooperative housing society manager, in a beige khadi kurta and a crisp white pajama, smiles as I enter the office on the Worli hill.

'This building came about in the early eighties. You were the first non-politician buyer, Anu. And now from what you tell me, you will be the first non-politician seller.' He has no idea of what I have been through.

'Let me know if there is an interested buyer, will you, Mr Swatantra Ram?'

Sold the property finally, losing the burden of possession—eleven cartons in all. Ten of them were gifted to Zaroorat, an NGO in Dharavi.

I was pretty sure I was heading to start yogi old-age homes in villages, bicycle riding for village girls, classes in English speaking, grooming the yogi way, by donating half or more of the income, if need be, that came from selling the house.

But nature was drumming another tune—the death, however temporary, of the working active arm.

In the last few years, wherever I was, I have researched on the various techniques that promise the same result but appear different in their approach. Hung out with Naga Baba of the Shaivite tantric tradition; other meditations took me away from crying, laughing into the 'drugless medicine' of Rajneesh the Mystic Rose; I learnt more about Craniosacral therapy; meditated in and managed a Buddhist meditation centre; used Vipassana to get an eagle-eye view on the natural phenomenon inside one; an Aghori Baba in the city opened up the Tantric sect of the cosmic harmony between mind and matter.

I tuned into my inner beat, and harmonized directly with consciousness. And my healing happened alongside silence and self-contemplation. A holistic approach and alternative yoga therapy, and mindfulness was used. I got to know who we are. Love is all there is.

I was in the city again and this time minus a house I could call my 'own'. My inner voice said: Write. Tell. Share.

What kind of place do I rent? Budget? My chartered accountant has a sly smile when he jokes that with with the sale of my house, and my earlier savings and investments from the glamour industry, there was more than enough.

'You can choose whatever monthly rent you want to pay, money no problem.'

Save some money for survival, so I do not have to draw money from teaching yoga. Teach yoga for free, teach yoga to set them free, is what I have in mind. Be You.

That is your work in the city, why you have been pulled back here.

Be like a leaf.

If you throw a leaf in water it flows away, taken by the flow of the water. Let life flow, without restriction. If you try to restrict it, the water will find its own way and take another path. If you allow the stream to carry you, its strength becomes yours. Leaving the past behind, live in the moment.

I am here today not just because I could not leave the people, but because of their love—they wanted me here. If I am alive today and living my dream it is only they who made that possible.

And just then Shanti interrupts my thoughts, 'Madam, a call for you. It is a Bollywood director...'

Epilogue

Years have passed since sanyas brought about alchemic changes within me.

The renunciation dress code done away with and the head no longer bare, I have internalized sanyas.

Women's empowerment, which I'd worked on all my life, has transcended to human empowerment.

Meagre needs and frugal wants had bred a lifestyle that allowed me to enjoy luxury as much as the bare minimum. The focus stayed on Karmayoga, wherever I was. Know thyself, forgive others. Flow.

I embraced my flaws. Acceptance.

Thankful for what I have. Gratitude. The shift in attitude aided my healing.

When managing a meditation centre in India's Wild West, Kutch, I found that my greatest pleasure came from helping others. In Mumbai, I work with slum kids. The healing module I had researched has metamorphosed into AnuFun Yoga, my way of teaching yoga. To see despondent slum kids spring up in joy has been immensely satisfying.

Compassion-in-action.

My life—a Shakespearean drama, a Greek mythology laced with Tantric wisdom.

Swamiglee was karmically out of my life. Thank you, Agapeto, for officially showing me the meaning of unconditional love. We'll meet in the astral plane, one moon.

Bliss is a start point.

I had searched for peace—I found peace, a pearl in my innermost being. Handcuffs and blindfolds of peace. Lotus bloom, from the spinal cord to the head.

Occasionally, I still hit the dance floor and boogie, but not a single Bollywood offer could entice me. Astral travel did, and you could change your dreams having seen the Other side...

But then who knows about the future? When your mind is open, anything is possible.

Life is a celebration.

Love is all there is.